ULTIMATE POCKET

FLAGS

OF THE

WORLD

DORLING KINDERSLEY
LONDON • NEW YORK • SYDNEY • MOSCOW

A DORLING KINDERSLEY BOOK

This book was produced in association with
The Flag Institute, Chester, UK.

We would like to dedicate this book to the late Dr William G Crampton, Director of
the Flag Institute, without whom it would not have been possible.

Project Editor Siobhán Ryan
Project Designer David Douglas

Designers Tony Cutting, Yahya El Droubie, Paul Williams

Editorial Contributors
Debra Clapson, Hayley Crockford, Michael Faul, Wim Jenkins,
Louise Keane, Nic Kynaston, Louisa Somerville

Managing Editor Lisa Thomas
Managing Art Editor Philip Lord
DTP Systems Manager Tokiko Morishima
Production Controller David Proffit

Additional Illustrations Ciárán Hughes

First published in Great Britain in 1997
by Dorling Kindersley Limited
9 Henrietta Street, London WC2E 8PS

A CIP catalogue record for this book is available from the British Library

ISBN 0-7513-1079-4

*Film output in England by Colourpath
Printed and bound in Italy by L.E.G.O.*

CONTENTS

NORTH & CENTRAL AMERICA

SOUTH AMERICA

AFRICA

EUROPE

AUSTRALASIA & OCEANIA

ASIA

INTRODUCTION

Flags are a part of everyday life. They are used by countries, provinces, cities, international bodies, organizations and companies.

EARLY FLAGS
The earliest known flags were used in China, to indicate different parts of the army. In Europe flags began with the Roman *vexillum*, a square flag used by Roman cavalry, from which the term 'vexillology' – the study of flags – originated. In the Middle Ages, heraldry became important as a means of identifying kings and lords. The distinctive coats of arms which developed were used as flags, and some still exist today.

FLAGS FOR IDENTIFICATION
The most significant development of flags was for use at sea. Ships flew flags for identification at a distance, and many of the rules of flag-use developed at sea. Some well-known flags were designed specifically for naval use, including the Dutch and Spanish flags *(see pages 123 & 138)* and the International code flags *(see page 238)*, which were used by ships to communicate with each other.

POLITICAL FLAGS
With the growth of independent nation states, flags have become more important in politics. Many newly-independent states choose flags based on those of the political parties which secured independence. Revolutionary movements usually have their own flags, and private and professional organizations are increasingly adopting flags.

This book deals with national, international and subnational flags, and national coats of arms, and is arranged continent by continent. Among national flags are the state ensign and flag, for government use only on sea and land; the civil ensign and flag, for private and commercial use; and the naval ensign, flown by warships. Subnational flags may be of states (USA), provinces (Canada), cantons (Switzerland), overseas territories or other such areas.

KEY FLAGS IN WORLD HISTORY
Throughout history certain flags have become the inspiration of others, starting with the Stars and Stripes in 1777 *(see pages 13–14)*; which has inspired more flags than any other. The same degree of influence has been exercised by the French *Tricolore* from 1794, *(see page 133)*, the Dutch Tricolour *(see page 123)* and its major derivative the Russian Tricolour *(see page 168)* which gave rise to most of the flags of eastern Europe. The next two pages summarize these key flags, whose 'offspring' can be seen throughout this book.

KEY FLAGS IN WORLD HISTORY

THE DUTCH
(*PRINSENVLAG*)
FLAG, c1600

This flag was adapted from the livery colours of William of Orange. During the 17th century, the orange was changed to red, leading to the development of the Russian Tricolour. Peter the Great of Russia was an admirer of the Dutch and adopted variations of their flag for Russia. The *Prinsenvlag* was also the inspiration of the former flag of South Africa and of flags used in New York (formerly New Amsterdam).

THE ANARCHIST
FLAG

This was first used during the French Revolution, as a variant of the Red Flag. The addition of black signified the idea of 'Liberty or Death'. In this form the flag was used in Haiti (1810) and influenced the German Tricolour of 1818. It was used throughout the 19th and 20th centuries as a political flag. It also gave rise to the flags of Angola *(see page 96)* and Fidel Castro, and is used by the Sandinistas in Nicaragua.

THE BRITISH
RED ENSIGN

The idea for this flag emerged in the 17th century, and in Britain gave rise to the red ensign for civil use, the blue ensign for government or state use and the white ensign for use on naval vessels. It is possible that the flag of the United Colonies 1775 *(see page 13)*, which eventually led to the Stars and Stripes, was a variant of this flag. In the mid-19th century the blue ensign began to be used by colonial governments. After independence many colonies continued to use a red or blue ensign. In Rhodesia, Fiji and Tuvalu, it was changed to light blue.

THE RED
FLAG

The Red Flag dates back to the French Revolution. It was used again in the Paris Commune (1870) and the Russian Revolution of 1905. It was not until the success of the 1917 Bolshevik Revolution that it became the flag of Russia and then the Soviet Union (1924). It was copied by communists in Vietnam, China and Africa *(see pages 208 & 217)*. Even though many communist regimes have now been supplanted, the Red Flag remains the flag of the extreme left and is widely used in one form or another as a left-wing party flag.

THE FLAG OF FRANCISCO DE MIRANDA, 1806

This was the first flag to symbolize emancipation from Spain in South America. A flag based on these colours was used for Colombia, Venezuela (and later Ecuador). The colours symbolized the blue ocean separating the Americas (red) from the 'tyrants' of Spain (yellow).

THE UNITED PROVINCES OF CENTRAL AMERICA, 1823

This is the flag of the Central American provinces which united to break away from Spain. It is not known whether the colours were derived from those of Argentina, or were indigenous to the region. Today, Nicaragua, and El Salvador use flags closely resembling this one.

THE FLAG OF MARCUS GARVEY, 1806

Marcus Garvey was a black activist who sought a new home for black people in Africa. He imagined the flag of 'Ethiopia' to be black, red and green. Garvey's movement was popular in the USA in the 1920s and subsequently in Jamaica. The colours inspired many African politicians after the Second World War.

THE RASTAFARIAN FLAG

The coronation of Ras Tafari (Haile Selassie) as Emperor of the real Ethiopia in 1930, led to the formation of the Rastafarian movement in the West Indies. They adopted the flag of Ethiopia and added black from the Garvey flag, often in the form of a lion. The colours have since used widely in Africa.

THE ARAB REVOLT FLAG, 1917

First used in the Hejaz it quickly spread to Syria, Iraq and Jordan. In 1920 the order of the stripes was changed to black-white-green. The red triangle symbolized the rule of the Hashemites and their descent from Muhammad. Today, King Hussein of Jordan is the only surviving ruler of this dynasty.

THE EGYPT LIBERATION MOVEMENT, 1953

This used the colours of the Arab Revolt flag and also introduced the eagle, said to have been the badge of Saladin. Originally it bore the then Egyptian emblem on its breast. In 1956 it was used as the basis for the United Arab Republic flag and since has been used as the basis for many Arab flags and arms.

Types of Flags

 Saltire

A diagonal cross stretching from corner to corner of the flag.

 Scandinavian cross

A cross with the upright set closer to the hoist than to the fly.

Cross

A cross is vertical, centrally placed and extends across the whole flag.

Coupled cross or Saltire

A cross or saltire which ends short of the edges of the flag is couped.

 Serration

A flag where two colours are separated by a serrated edge.

 Quartered

A flag divided into four equal sections of differing design.

Fimbriated

A narrow strip of colour separating two broader stripes or larger areas.

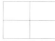 Bicolour

A flag of two stripes of different colours, either horizontal or vertical.

Tricolour

A flag of three stripes of three colours, either horizontal or vertical.

 Triangle

A flag divided by a triangle of a different colour, usually at the hoist.

 Counter-changed

A charge placed on a line where two colours meet, which reverses them.

 Bordered

A flag where the central colour is surrounded by a different colour.

PARTS OF THE FLAG

As with every field of knowledge, specialist terms are used to describe flags and their usage.

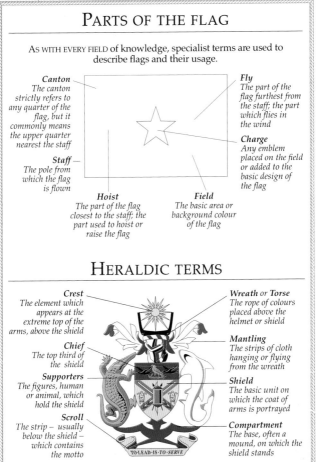

Canton
The canton strictly refers to any quarter of the flag, but it commonly means the upper quarter nearest the staff

Staff
The pole from which the flag is flown

Hoist
The part of the flag closest to the staff; the part used to hoist or raise the flag

Fly
The part of the flag furthest from the staff; the part which flies in the wind

Charge
Any emblem placed on the field or added to the basic design of the flag

Field
The basic area or background colour of the flag

HERALDIC TERMS

Crest
The element which appears at the extreme top of the arms, above the shield

Chief
The top third of the shield

Supporters
The figures, human or animal, which hold the shield

Scroll
The strip – usually below the shield – which contains the motto

Wreath or Torse
The rope of colours placed above the helmet or shield

Mantling
The strips of cloth hanging or flying from the wreath

Shield
The basic unit on which the coat of arms is portrayed

Compartment
The base, often a mound, on which the shield stands

TO·LEAD·IS·TO·SERVE

CANADA

Ratio: 1:2   Adopted: 15 February 1965   Usage: National and Civil

A stylized maple leaf has been Canada's national emblem for over 150 years

White represents the snowy north of Canada

Red represents the sacrifice made by Canadians during the First World War

NORTH AMERICA

CANADA BECAME A NATION in 1867 when four colonies united. Later, six other provinces and two territories joined the Confederation.

For many years Canada was without a national flag and used the British Red Ensign with the Canadian shield in the fly. In the early 1960s, pressure began to grow for a distinctive flag. The initial contender, known as 'Pearson's Pennant', used maple leaves to represent Canada and a blue bar on either side representing the Pacific and Atlantic oceans.

THE NEW MAPLE LEAF FLAG
Pearson's Pennant did not meet with universal approval, and consensus was only reached on the idea of the maple leaf and on the use of the national colours. The result was the 'Maple Leaf Flag' which was adopted by Parliament in 1965. However, both the Union Jack and old red ensign remain in use.

CANADIAN RED ENSIGN

The Union Jack has been retained to symbolize Canada's link with the Commonwealth

The quarters of the shield represent England, France, Scotland and Ireland – the homelands of many Canadian people

10

Canada – Provincial flags

THE DATE WHEN EACH province joined the Confederation is shown below the province name.

 ALBERTA
1905

The shield dates from 1907 and was placed on a blue field to make a flag in 1967. The shield depicts a scene from the vast wheat lands of the west under St George's Cross.

 BRITISH COLUMBIA
1871

This flag, adopted in 1960, is an armorial banner of the arms, granted in 1906. The sun placed over heraldic waters, represents the province's position on the west coast.

 MANITOBA
1870

The flag is intended to recall and to preserve the old Canadian Red Ensign, with Manitoba's shield, depicting a buffalo on a rock, in the fly. It was adopted in 1966.

 NEWFOUNDLAND & LABRADOR
1949

The colours of the flag attempt to represent all aspects of the province, such as snow, ice and the sea. The design is intended to recall the Union Jack, the previous flag.

 NEW BRUNSWICK
1867

Another armorial banner, authorized in 1965. The galley ship stands for shipbuilding, once an important industry, and the lion represents New Brunswick's ties to Britain.

 NOVA SCOTIA
1867

Theoretically the oldest flag of a British Dominion. 'Nova Scotia' means New Scotland. Its flag is a St Andrew's Cross in reversed colours, with the Scottish Royal Arms.

 ONTARIO
1867

The flag was adopted in 1965 and also attempts to recall and preserve the Canadian Red Ensign. The shield is from the arms of 1868 and was the first design to use a maple leaf.

 PRINCE EDWARD ISLAND
1873

The flag is a banner of the arms granted in 1905. It depicts an island, with a great British oak and its 'descendants', under the protection of a British lion.

QUÉBEC
1867

The flag is a modernized version of an old French-Canadian flag known as the *Fleurdelysé* and was adopted in 1948. The *fleur-de-lis* flower is symbolic of France. It is the best-known of the provincial flags.

SASKATCHEWAN
1905

Adopted in 1969, the flag of Saskatchewan combines the provincial shield with the floral emblem, the western red lily. The colours stand for the forests of the north and grain fields of the south.

NORTHWEST TERRITORIES
1870

The flag was chosen from competition entries in 1969. It contains the shield from the arms adopted in 1956. The colours represent the lakes and waters in blue and the snow in white.

YUKON TERRITORY
1898

Accepted as the territorial flag in 1967, the flag uses the whole coat of arms adopted in 1956. The colours symbolize the green *taiga* forests, the white winter snows and the blue northern waters.

CAPE BRETON ISLAND

This flag was adopted in 1994 for use in Cape Breton, which is part of Nova Scotia. It was the winning design in a competition. It shows a stylized island rising from the sea, with a bald eagle flying above.

LABRADOR

The stripes represent the snows, waters and forests of Labrador, which is part of Newfoundland Province. The three sprigs on the spruce twig denote the three main races who live in the territory.

GOVERNOR-GENERAL OF CANADA

Flags for the Governor-General usually contain the British Royal Crest. The Canadian one, which dates from 1981, has its own crest, in which the lion holds a maple leaf.

HM THE QUEEN OF CANADA

From early in her reign, the Queen began to adopt royal standards for use in her various dominions, based on their own arms. The Canadian version dates from 1962.

UNITED STATES OF AMERICA

Ratio: *10:19* Adopted: *1960* Usage: *National and Civil*

The 50 stars stand for each of the current states of the Union

13 stripes stand for the original 13 colonies which formed the United States

If a new state joins the Union a star is added the following 4 July

NORTH AMERICA

THE UNITED STATES was formed when 13 colonies rose against the British in 1775. They declared their independence from Britain on 4 July 1776.

The first flag used by the Americans was an adaptation of the British Red Ensign, known as the 'Grand Union Flag,' *(see page 14)*. From this developed the distinctive 'Stars and Stripes', as it known today, which still has the 13 stripes for each of the original colonies to join the Union, and a star for each state which is now part of the USA. The latest star was added on 4 July 1960, after Hawaii joined the USA in 1959.

A TRULY NATIONAL FLAG
The flag of 1777 *(see page 14)*, marked a break with old colonial ties. It became the first of a new kind of flag, one which was truly a national flag in the modern sense. Its basic

design and colour combination was soon copied by other new nations.

The Stars and Stripes is an all-purpose flag, but the USA is rich in flags of many other kinds.

THE PRESIDENT'S STANDARD
The Presidential standard, in use today, contains the President's version of the national arms, and a ring of 50 stars. The coat of arms depicts a spread eagle holding a shield in the style of the Stars and Stripes, 13 arrows and 13 olive leaves, indicating the country is prepared for either war or peace. The motto *'E Pluribus Unum'*, meaning 'Out of many, one' reflects the federal nature of the United States.

13

USA – Historical flags

THE FLAGS OF THE War of Independence and of the Civil War still have an influence on the American flags of today.

THE GRAND UNION FLAG

The first American flag was adapted from the British Red Ensign of the time. It was known as the 'Grand Union Flag', i.e. of the Union of 13 colonies. These were represented by the 13 stripes of red and white. The flag was introduced in December 1775 for use on land and at sea.

THE FIRST STARS AND STRIPES

On 14 June 1777 the Union Jack was removed from the flag in favour of a blue canton with 13 stars, representing a new constellation, which now also represented the United States. This was the first use of stars in this way, and set a precedent for many later flags.

THE FLAG OF 1795

When two new states joined the Union in 1795, two new stars and two new stripes were added to the flag, making 15 stripes and 15 stars. This set a precedent for adding new stripes and stars when each new state joined the Union. The flag soon became known as the 'Star Spangled Banner'.

THE FLAG OF 1818

Five new states were formed after 1795, but a new flag was not designed until 1817 when Congress decreed that in future only new stars would be added and it would revert to 13 stripes, in order to preserve the appearance of the flag. The new stars were added on 4 July 1818, and this system has been followed ever since.

THE STARS AND BARS

When the Southern states seceded from the Union in 1860, a new flag for the Confederacy was hoisted on 4 March 1861, was known as the 'Stars and Bars'. It originally had 7 stars, but these increased to 13 in the course of 1861, as more states joined the Confederacy.

THE BATTLE FLAG OR 'FLAG OF THE SOUTH'

The Battle Flag with its distinctive saltire on a red field (Southern Cross) was introduced in September 1861, specifically for use in battle. On land it was square with a white border, but the rectangular naval version, without a border, is now accepted as 'The Flag of the South'.

USA – State flags

THE DATE WHEN each state joined the Union is shown below the state name.

ALABAMA
1819

The red saltire is intended to recall the Southern Cross or Battle Flag of the Confederate States. The flag was adopted in 1895 and is the only completely square state flag.

ALASKA
1959

The flag was designed by an Indian schoolboy in 1926, when Alaska was still a territory. It depicts the Plough and the northern Pole star. Gold also represents Alaska's mineral reserves.

ARIZONA
1912

The red and yellow rays recall the period of Spanish rule and the copper star stands for mineral riches. The flag was designed locally and adopted in 1927.

ARKANSAS
1836

The flag recalls the Southern Cross. The lower stars represent former colonial powers and the upper star stands for the Confederacy. The flag was adopted in 1913.

CALIFORNIA
1850

The flag is based on that of the California Republic declared at Sonora in 1846; it did not become the state flag until 1911. It depicts a grizzly bear and a star for freedom.

COLORADO
1876

The C-shaped emblem contains the colours of Spain, which once laid claim to this area. The gold ball also represents the state's mineral riches. The flag was adopted in 1911.

CONNECTICUT
1788

The arms date back to the seal of 1784, and the blue field to the Civil War period, when the flag was a Union colour. This design was adopted in 1897.

DELAWARE
1787

The arms date back to 1777 and the flag, adopted in 1913, includes the date Delaware joined the Union. The colours recall the uniforms worn during the War of Independence.

DISTRICT OF
COLUMBIA
1791

The flag of the Federal District of
Columbia is based on a banner of the
arms of the Washington family,
which originated in England and
dates back to 1592. It was adopted in
1938 by a Congress Commission.

FLORIDA
1845

This is another flag which recalls the
Southern Cross used by the
Confederacy during the Civil War.
The original flag, adopted in 1868,
had only the seal, the red saltire was
added in 1900.

GEORGIA
1788

Here the whole Confederate
Southern Cross flag was added to
the fly in 1956, replacing the red and
white Stars and Bars. The state seal,
depicting a soldier with a drawn
sword, dates back to 1799.

HAWAII
1959

The state flag, originally
representing the independent
kingdom, was adopted in 1845. The
Union Jack recalls a flag given to the
King by an army officer in 1793. The
stripes stand for the main islands.

IDAHO
1890

The flag was originally a military
colour and bears the state seal in the
centre; beneath it is a scroll with the
state's name. The flag in this form
was adopted in 1927, with new
specifications in 1957.

ILLINOIS
1818

Created in 1915, the central emblem
of the Illinois flag, depicts elements
from the state seal, including a bald
eagle and a shield of the Stars and
Stripes. The name was added
beneath this in 1970.

INDIANA
1816

The flag was the winning entry in a
design competition held in 1916, and
was officially adopted in 1917. The
stars in two arcs are for the original
states and the subsequent ones.

IOWA
1846

The red, white and blue colours
stand for French Louisiana, of which
Iowa was once a part. In the centre is
the seal of 1847. The flag was
adopted in this form in 1921.

Kansas
1861

The flag of Kansas follows a very common seal and name pattern. The original flag of 1925 had the seal, recalling settlement and agriculture, and a sunflower – the state flower. The name was added in 1963.

Kentucky
1792

Another flag derived from the militia colours. The flag was adopted in 1918 and regularized in 1962. Like many state flags it contains the seal, the state name and a wreath of golden rod, the state flower.

Louisiana
1812

The pelican, representing self-sacrifice and the state's role as a protector, has long been the badge of Louisiana, but the flag was only adopted in 1912. The Acadians or 'Cajuns' also have their own flag.

Maine
1820

The flag dates from 1909 when the arms, adopted in 1820, were placed on a blue field. The star and motto recall Maine's northerly location. It was the northernmost state of the union, until Michigan joined in 1837.

Maryland
1788

This is the only flag which is a true heraldic banner, reproducing the arms of the Baltimore family, once the 'proprietors' of the state. Each side of the family is represented by two quarters. It was adopted in 1904.

Massachusetts
1788

The flag was originally adopted in 1908 and revised in 1971, replacing a pine tree with the coat of arms adopted in 1780. The arms, depicting an Amerindian holding a bow, now appears on both sides of the flag.

Michigan
1837

The arms was adopted in 1832, and placed on a blue field to make the state flag in 1911. The mottoes mean 'I will defend', and 'If you seek a pleasant peninsula, look about you'.

Minnesota
1858

The motto on this flag 'The North Star', was retained from when the state was the northernmost in the Union. The flag was originally adopted in 1893 and revised in 1957.

MISSISSIPPI
1817

MISSOURI
1821

The flag of Mississippi was adopted in 1894. It combines both the Confederacy's Southern Cross with the stripes of its first flag, the Stars and Bars, although on the flag of Mississippi the upper stripe is blue.

The colours of the flag recall when the region was under French control. The 24 stars stand for Missouri being the 24th state to join the Union. Within the seal itself are another 24 stars. The flag was adopted in 1913.

MONTANA
1889

NEBRASKA
1867

The flag is derived from the former state militia colours, while the motto, 'Gold and Silver' is in Spanish, recalling Spain's claim to the area. The flag was adopted in 1905 and had the name added in 1981.

The flag of Nebraska was adopted in 1925 and uses the seal which was adopted in 1867. This depicts an allegorical landscape, symbolic of the state's agricultural and industrial development.

NEVADA
1864

NEW HAMPSHIRE
1788

The flag emerged from a design competition and was adopted in 1929. It was revised in 1991 and the state name was placed underneath boughs of the sage bush and the star, which represents the state.

The design was adopted in 1909, making use of the seal, which dates back to 1775. It depicts a ship, the *Raleigh*, being built on the stocks at the town of Portsmouth during the War of Independence.

NEW JERSEY
1787

NEW MEXICO
1912

The buff field recalls the uniforms worn during the War of Independence. The flag with the arms was adopted in 1896 and made generally available in 1938.

This most distinctive flag was adopted in 1925 and uses the sun symbol of the *Zia Pueblo* Indians, while the colours represent the Spanish colonial era.

NEW YORK
1788

NORTH CAROLINA
1789

The flag dates originally from flags used in the War of Independence, but in this form only from 1901. Prior to that the flag had a buff field. The two figures symbolize liberty and justice. The coat of arms dates from 1777.

The original flag was adopted in 1861 at the outbreak of the Civil War, and was in the same colours as the Stars and Bars. The present design dates from 1885. It contains the initials of the state in the blue stripe.

NORTH DAKOTA
1889

OHIO
1803

The flag was originally used by the state militia, the North Dakota Infantry, and was adopted in 1911, almost without alteration, explaining its squarish shape. In the centre is a version of the national arms.

The pennant-shaped flag of Ohio is derived from a cavalry guidon of the Civil War period. The 17 stars recall that Ohio was the 17th state to join the union and the circle or 'O' refers to the state's initial.

OKLAHOMA
1907

OREGON
1859

The basic design emerged from a design competition and was adopted in 1925. The name was added in 1941. The Amerindian emblems, all symbols of peace, recall the previous name, 'Indian Territory'.

This is now the only state flag with a different design on its reverse. The obverse shows the seal within 33 stars, the state's name and its date of admission. The reverse shows a beaver. It was adopted in 1925.

PENNSYLVANIA
1787

RHODE ISLAND
1790

The coat of arms of the state was adopted in 1777 and regularized in 1875. It was placed on a blue field to make the flag in 1907. The shield is supported by two horses.

The anchor, symbolic of hope, has long been the emblem of Rhode Island. The flag, based on a War of Independence flag, was adopted in 1877 and modified in 1897.

South Carolina
1788

The flag was adopted in 1861 at the very start of the Civil War, but contains emblems used during the War of Independence and also used in the state arms. The central palmetto is the state tree.

 South Dakota
1889

The flag of South Dakota was adopted in 1963 on the basis of previous models and had the former motto 'The Sunshine State' around the seal. This was changed to 'The Mount Rushmore State' in 1992.

 Tennessee
1796

The three stars indicate that the state was the third to join the Union after the original 13 states, whilst its general appearance recalls the Battle Flag or Southern Cross. The flag was adopted in 1905.

 Texas
1845

The flag copies the colours of the Stars and Stripes, but with only one star, which dates back to one on the plain blue flag of the Republic of Texas. It was adopted in 1839 and retained after Texas joined the Union.

 Utah
1896

The beehive in the flag recalls the emblem of the Mormon state of Deseret, located in Utah and the date recalls their settlement of the region. The present flag dates from 1911, and uses the seal adopted in 1896.

 Vermont
1791

The arms, including the Lone Pine emblem, date back to when Vermont was independent from 1777–91. The present flag, based on the former militia flag, was adopted in 1923. The state name appears on a scroll.

 Virginia
1788

The state arms was adopted in 1776. The seal, showing a victorious warrior, was placed on the flag in 1861 at the start of the Civil War. The design has been used ever since.

 Washington
1889

Washington is known as 'The Evergreen State' and this is reflected by its flag. It is the only state with a green flag. The seal dates from 1889 and was placed on the flag in 1923.

WEST VIRGINIA
1863

 WISCONSIN
1848

The coat of arms dates from 1863 when West Virginia seceded from Virginia. The current version of the flag was adopted in 1929 and has the arms within a wreath of rhododendron, the state flower.

The flag is derived from the militia colours of the Union in 1863. It depicts the state seal, supported by a miner and a sailor. The shield also recalls mining and sailing. The name and the date were added in 1980.

 WYOMING
1890

 AMERICAN SAMOA

The flag emerged from a design competition and was adopted in 1917. The flag has been revised several times, at one time the buffalo containing the arms faced the fly. The colours recall the national flag.

A self-governing US dependency, American Samoa's flag contains many associations with its guardian state, not only in the colours of the flag, but also the emblem, which is an American bald eagle.

 GUAM

 NORTHERN MARIANA ISLANDS

The flag was designed locally and adopted in 1917. In the centre of the flag, in the US colours, is the seal of the territory, which depicts an idealized landscape. The flag can only be flown with the US flag.

The original flag was adopted in 1972, but has undergone several modifications, including the addition of the flower-wreath. It also depicts a grey *latte* stone representing the islands' *Chamorro* culture.

 PUERTO RICO

 VIRGIN ISLANDS (US)

The resemblance of this flag to that of Cuba is no coincidence, since the two were designed at the same time, by the same activists. This version was adopted in 1952.

The flag dates from 1921 and uses part of the US seal, with the initials of the islands. The three arrows in one claw stand for the main islands; in the other claw is an olive branch.

MEXICO

Ratio: 4:7   Adopted: 2 November 1821   Usage: National and Civil

The basic design is derived from the French Tricolore

Red, white and green are the colours of the national liberation army in Mexico

The coat of arms incorporates the badge of Mexico City

NORTH AMERICA

MEXICO WAS CONQUERED by Spain in the 16th century, but broke away in 1821 to form a Central American state. It became a republic in 1822.

France was the inspiration of those who detached Mexico from Spain in 1821 and they devised a new tricolour based on the flag of the liberation army. At that time the Italian tricolour was not in use.

The flag now contains the coat of arms, in order to distinguish it from that of Italy.

THE AZTEC INHERITANCE

The central emblem is the Aztec pictogram for Tenochtitlán (now Mexico City), the centre of their empire. It recalls the legend which inspired the Aztecs to settle on what was originally a lake-island.

The form of the coat of arms was most recently revised in 1968.

ARMS OF MEXICO

Aztec legend held that they should found their city on the spot where they saw an eagle on a cactus, eating a snake

The lake with an island, represents Tenochtitlán

Ribbon in the national colours

GUATEMALA

Ratio: 5:8 Adopted: *17 August 1871* Usage: *National and State*

Blue and white are the colours of the original flag of the United Provinces of Central America

The coat of arms was adopted in 1968

NORTH AMERICA

GUATEMALA DECLARED independence at the same time as Mexico and, in 1823, became part of a union with the other Central American states.

In Guatemala, the Central American flag *(see page 7)* was used until 1851 when a pro-Spanish faction took over and added the Spanish colours of red and yellow to the flag. On 17 August 1871 the original colours were restored, but in vertical, rather than horizontal stripes and with a new coat of arms.

THE QUETZAL BIRD
The new coat of arms shows the quetzal, Guatemala's most famous bird, standing on a scroll giving the date of the Declaration of Independence. The present form of the arms was adopted in 1968.

When used at sea for civil purposes, the flag does not contain the arms.

ARMS OF GUATEMALA

The date of the Declaration of Independence

Rifles and swords represent defence of freedom

The quetzal bird with its distinctive tail-feathers is a symbol of liberty

BELIZE

Ratio: *3:5* Adopted: *21 September 1981* Usage: *National and Civil*

The coat of arms was granted in 1907

The 50 leaves recall 1950, the year the PUP came to power

Blue is the party colour of the PUP

Red stripes were added to denote the colour of the opposition party

NORTH AMERICA

BELIZE WAS originally known as British Honduras, a colony formed in 1862 from settlements on the coast of Guatemala.

British Honduras obtained a coat of arms on 28 January 1907, which formed the basis of the badge used on British ensigns. The coat of arms recalls the logging industry which first led to British settlement there.

From 1968 onwards an unofficial national flag was in use. It was blue with a modified version of the arms – minus the Union Jack – on a white disc in the centre. The colours were those of the People's United Party (PUP). Around the arms was a wreath of 50 leaves, recalling 1950, when the PUP came to prominence.

On independence in 1981, the flag was retained but red was added to stand for the opposition party.

ARMS OF BELIZE

The figures, tools and the mahogany tree represent the logging industry

Wreath of 50 leaves

National motto – 'Sub Umbra Floreo' *meaning* 'I Flourish in the Shade'

EL SALVADOR

Ratio: 3:5 Adopted: 17 May 1912 Usage: National and State

The flag is modelled on the flag of the United Provinces of Central America

The emblem is surrounded by the national flags of the members of the United Provinces of Central America

The title of the state while it was part of the United Provinces of Central America surrounds the emblem

NORTH AMERICA

Guatemala Honduras
EL SALVADOR

EL SALVADOR'S FLAG recalls the colours of the United Provinces of Central America, used following independence from Spain in 1823.

The flag of Central America (*see page 7*) was used as the national flag until 1865, when a flag based on the Stars and Stripes was adopted, with blue and white stripes and a red canton containing nine stars.

In 1912 the original design was re-adopted, with the arms of El Salvador in the centre.

TRIANGLES AND VOLCANOES

The coat of arms is similar to those of the United Provinces of Central America. The emblem is based on the Masonic triangle for equality, and depicts the five original provinces with five volcanoes. Around the triangle are five national flags and a wreath, tied in the national colours.

ARMS OF EL SALVADOR

A triangle representing equality

The motto of Central America – 'Dios, Union, Libertad' meaning 'God, Union, Liberty'

The Cap of Liberty

Five volcanoes representing the original united provinces

HONDURAS

Ratio: *1:2*   Adopted: *16 February 1866*   Usage: *National and Civil*

The colours and pattern are the same as the flag of the United Provinces of Central America

Five stars recall the five original members of the United Provinces of Central America

NORTH AMERICA

HONDURAS WAS ONE of the Spanish colonies which formed the United Provinces of Central America in 1823. It became independent in 1838.

In 1823 Honduras joined the United Provinces of Central America and adopted their flag *(see page 7)*. In 1866 it was amended; five blue stars were placed in the centre to represent the five original Central American provinces. The state flag has the arms of Honduras in the centre in place of the stars.

The arms was created in 1838 and revised in 1935. The central feature is a pyramid in Maya style rising from the sea. Around this is a band with the name of the state and the date of the Declaration of Independence. Beneath it is a landscape strewn with allegorical items representing mineral and timber industries.

ARMS OF HONDURAS

The cornucopias are symbolic of prosperity and agricultural wealth

A Maya pyramid

The landscape depicts mines, mining tools, forests and logging tools

NICARAGUA

Ratio: 3:5 Adopted: 4 September 1908 Usage: National and Civil

Apart from the text round the arms, the flag is identical to that of the United Provinces of Central America

Arms of Nicaragua

'America Central' recalls the United Provinces of Central America

NORTH AMERICA

NICARAGUA DECLARED independence from Spain in 1821. It was a member of the United Provinces of Central America from 1823 to 1838.

The flag and the arms of Nicaragua in use today are the most similar to those used by the United Provinces of Central America. The triangle, volcanoes, rising sun, Cap of Liberty, and rainbow all appeared on the original emblem. The coat of arms used today contains the name of the state, *Republica de Nicaragua*, whereas

in 1823 the title was *Provincias Unidas del Centro de America.*

The decision to revert to the emblems used by the United Provinces of Central America was taken in 1908 and reflected Nicaragua's aspirations for the rebirth of the political entity formed by the five nations.

ARMS OF NICARAGUA

The five volcanoes represent the original five member states

The rays of the sun and the rainbow are symbolic of the bright future

The Cap of Liberty represents national freedom

COSTA RICA

Ratio: 3:5   Adopted: *29 September 1848*   Usage: *National and State*

Blue and white were the colours of the original flag of the United Provinces of Central America

Red, white and blue recall the colours of the French Tricolore

NORTH AMERICA

COSTA RICA WAS a signatory to the Declaration of Independence from Spain in 1821, joining the United Provinces of Central America (1823–1838).

The Central American flag remained in use in Costa Rica until 1848 when, in response to events in France, it was decided to incorporate the French colours into the national flag. This was done by adding a central red stripe. The coat of arms was also revised and placed in the centre of the flag. In 1906, it was placed in a white disc on the red stripe, and later on an oval, set towards the hoist.

The coat of arms depicts the isthmus between the Pacific Ocean and the Caribbean Sea. The stars stand for the seven provinces and the Central American union is recalled by *'America Central'* on the upper scroll.

ARMS OF COSTA RICA

'America Central' recalls the former United Provinces of Central America

The Caribbean Sea

Seven stars for the seven provinces

Three volcanoes on the isthmus

The Pacific Ocean

PANAMA

Ratio: 2:3 Adopted: 3 November 1903 Usage: *National and Civil*

Although inspired by the Stars and Stripes, the stars and quarters are said to represent the two main political parties

Red was the colour of the Conservatives and blue that of the Liberals

White symbolizes peace in the country

NORTH AMERICA

PANAMA, ORIGINALLY a province of Colombia, was detached in 1903 to secure the building of the Panama Canal within a US-controlled zone.

The first flag, proposed in 1903, consisted of seven horizontal stripes of red and yellow, with a blue canton containing two golden suns, joined by a narrow line to depict the oceans to be united by the Panama Canal.

However this was not accepted by the Panamanian leader, Manuel A. Guerrero, whose family designed a new flag. Although clearly modelled on the US flag, the stars and quarters are said to stand for the rival political parties, and the white for the peace in which they operate.

The coat of arms reflects Panama's transition from civil war to peace, and the increased prosperity this promised the people.

ARMS OF PANAMA

The shield depicts tools, weapons, a cornucopia and a winged wheel, which together symbolize a move from war, to peace and prosperity

The national motto – 'Pro Mundi Benefico' meaning 'For the benefit of the World'

The northern and southern hemispheres joined by the Panama Canal

JAMAICA

Ratio: 1:2   Adopted: 6 August 1962   Usage: National and Civil

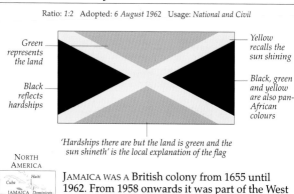

Green represents the land

Black reflects hardships

Yellow recalls the sun shining

Black, green and yellow are also pan-African colours

'Hardships there are but the land is green and the sun shineth' is the local explanation of the flag

NORTH AMERICA

JAMAICA WAS A British colony from 1655 until 1962. From 1958 onwards it was part of the West Indies Federation, which was dissolved in 1962.

The present design emerged from those sent in by the public in a national competition. It was originally designed with vertical stripes, but this was considered too similar to the Tanganyikan flag, and so the saltire was substituted.

The coat of arms, based on those granted to Jamaica on 3 February 1663, is among the oldest granted to

a British colony. It was used on the former British flags of Jamaica.

THE QUEEN'S STANDARD

The flag for HM Queen Elizabeth II, was introduced after independence. It contains a banner of the arms, with the Queen's Cypher in the centre. The shield depicts the red Cross of St George charged with pineapples.

BANNER OF THE QUEEN OF JAMAICA

St George's Cross

The Royal Cypher is enclosed within a chaplet of roses

The four pineapples and cross are taken from the Arms of Jamaica

CUBA

Ratio: 1:2   Adopted: *20 May 1902*   Usage: *National and Civil*

'La Estrella Solitaria' – the Lone Star

The design is based on the US Stars and Stripes

The triangle comes from the Masonic symbol for equality

NORTH AMERICA

CUBA, the only communist state in the Americas, was a Spanish colony until 1898, when it was ceded to the USA. It gained independence in 1902.

The flag was designed in 1848 for the liberation movement, which sought to detach Cuba from Spain and make it into a state of the USA. The Lone Star represented another star which would be added to 'the splendid North American constellation'. The triangle is derived from the Masonic symbol for equality, while the five stripes stand for the five provinces of the time. The flag was briefly hoisted in 1850 at Cardenas, but was not officially adopted until 1902, when independence was granted by the USA.

Another flag from the 19th century is that of Carlos Manuel de Céspedes, used by the independence movement of 1868–78. It is now used as the Jack of the Cuban navy.

FLAG OF CÉSPEDES

The flag is like that of Chile with the blue and red reversed

This flag was also modelled on the Stars and Stripes, using the same colours: blue, red and white and a star in the canton

31

BAHAMAS

Ratio: 1:2 Adopted: 10 July 1973 Usage: National

Black
represents
the strength
of the people

Blue
recalls the
Caribbean
Sea

Yellow reflects the islands' sandy beaches

NORTH
AMERICA

ORIGINALLY A PIRATE BASE, the Bahamas became a
formal British colony in 1783. It did not achieve
independence until 10 July 1973.

The colours of the flag are intended
to represent the aquamarine seas
around the islands and their golden
sands. The flag is based on designs
by the Bahamian people. Many of
those submitted also included the
idea of sunrise, which has been
incorporated into the coat of arms.

The Bahamas Civil Ensign (flown
by merchant ships) is often seen,

since many ships are registered in
the Bahamas. The flag is based on
the British Red Ensign – red with a
Bahamian national flag in the
canton– but is distinguished by the
white cross, like the Cross of St
George, across the red field.

The Bahamas has many other flags
including one for the specific use of
the Prime Minister.

BAHAMAS CIVIL ENSIGN

The national flag is
placed in the canton

The civil ensign is
distinguished from
government and
naval ensigns by its
red field

HAITI

Ratio: 3:5   Adopted: *18 May 1803*   Usage: *National and Civil*

For official and state purposes the flag is charged with the national arms on a central white disc

Blue and red are taken from the French Tricolore

NORTH AMERICA

HAITI BECAME A French colony in 1697, but in 1803 a rebellion broke out. Independence was granted on 1 January 1804.

The blue and red of the flag were retained after a French *Tricolore* was torn up by the rebel Jean-Jacques Dessalines in 1803. The two parts were stitched together horizontally to make a new flag.

However a rival flag of vertical black and red panels was also used at various times, most recently in the period from 1964–86, during the regime of the Duvalier family.

Since 1843 the flag for official and state use has had the arms on a white panel in the centre. The coat of arms depicts a trophy of weapons ready to defend freedom, and a royal palm topped with a Cap of Liberty for the country's independence.

ARMS OF HAITI

The Cap of Liberty

The royal palm symbolizes independence

Weapons reflect the people's willingness to defend their liberty

The national motto – 'L'Union Fait La Force' meaning 'Union is Strength'

DOMINICAN REPUBLIC

Ratio: 2:3   Adopted: 6 November 1844   Usage: National and State

Blue and red are taken from the flag of Haiti, which once controlled the Dominican Republic

The coat of arms only appears on the flag for national and state use

The cross of the Trinitarian independence movement

NORTH
AMERICA

A SPANISH COLONY, briefly occupied by Haiti (1820–44), the Trinitarian movement was formed to free the country. It was liberated in 1844.

The flag was designed by the leader of the Trinitarians. He altered the layout of the blue and red of the Haitian flag, placing a large white cross over it to symbolize faith.

A DISTINCTIVE NATIONAL FLAG
To create distinct flags for state and civil use, the coat of arms, adopted in

1844, was placed on the state flag. The civil flag, on both land and sea, does not carry the arms.

The arms depicts a Bible open at the first chapter of St John's Gospel. This is placed on a trophy of national flags, on a shield of the same design. The Trinitarian motto is above this and the name of the state below.

ARMS OF THE DOMINICAN REPUBLIC

Gospel of St John, a Trinitarian emblem

The lower scroll contains the state title

The password of the Trinitarian movement – 'Dios, Patria, Libertad' ('God, Country, Freedom')

ST KITTS & NEVIS

Ratio: 2:3   Adopted: *19 September 1983*   Usage: *National and Civil*

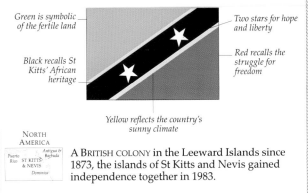

Green is symbolic of the fertile land

Two stars for hope and liberty

Black recalls St Kitts' African heritage

Red recalls the struggle for freedom

Yellow reflects the country's sunny climate

NORTH
AMERICA

A BRITISH COLONY in the Leeward Islands since 1873, the islands of St Kitts and Nevis gained independence together in 1983.

The flag was the winning entry in a local competition which attracted 258 entries, and was the work of a student, Edrice Lewis. It was she who gave what is now the official interpretation of the flag – that its colours stand for the fertile land, year-round sunshine, the struggle for freedom and the African heritage. The two stars stand for hope and

liberty, not for the islands of St Kitts and Nevis.

THE FLAG OF NEVIS

The island of Nevis has a flag of its own, which is bright yellow, with a stylized image of Nevis Peak. The national flag is in the canton.

St Kitts also has an ensign for the Coast Guard.

THE FLAG OF NEVIS

National flag in canton

Yellow for year-long sunshine

A graphic representation of Nevis Peak, a cone-shaped mountain in the centre of the island

ANTIGUA & BARBUDA

Ratio: 2:3   Adopted: *27 February 1967*   Usage: *National and Civil*

Black recalls the islands' African heritage

The rising sun represents a new era

The V-shape is the symbol of victory

White symbolizes hope

Blue represents the Caribbean Sea

NORTH AMERICA

ANTIGUA & BARBUDA

Puerto Rico

FROM 1632 UNTIL formal independence was granted in 1981, Antigua and its neighbour Barbuda were British colonies.

The flag dates from the achievement of self-government in 1967 and was the winning design in a competition which over 600 local people entered.

THE SYMBOLISM OF THE FLAG

The designer, Reginald Samuel, interpreted it as representing the sun rising against the background of the peoples' African heritage in a new era. The overall V-shape stands for victory. It is on a red background which symbolizes the dynamism of the population. Blue is for the sea and white is for hope.

THE NEW NATIONAL FLAG

The flag was retained unchanged when Antigua became independent.

Barbuda does not have a separate flag, although there is one for Redonda, an uninhabited island whose 'throne' is claimed by several rival 'monarchs'.

THE NATIONAL ARMS

The coat of arms was granted in 1977 and depicts a shield with a sugar mill, once the primary industry, on a background of white and blue waves. Above this is a sun on a black background. The shield stands on a sea island. The crest is a pineapple from the arms of the former colony of the Leeward Islands, of which Antigua was once a part. Beneath is a scroll with the national motto – 'Each endeavouring, all achieving'.

DOMINICA

Ratio: *1:2*   Adopted: *3 November 1978*   Usage: *National and Civil*

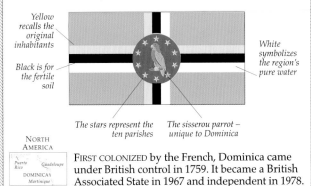

Yellow recalls the original inhabitants

Black is for the fertile soil

White symbolizes the region's pure water

The stars represent the ten parishes

The sisserou parrot – unique to Dominica

NORTH
AMERICA

Puerto Rico   Guadeloupe

DOMINICA
Martinique

FIRST COLONIZED by the French, Dominica came under British control in 1759. It became a British Associated State in 1967 and independent in 1978.

The flag adopted in 1978 features the national bird emblem, the sisserou parrot, which also appears on the coat of arms granted 21 July 1961. This parrot is unique to Dominica. It is an endangered species; only a few pairs remain.

The green field represents the lush vegetation of the island. The cross represents the Trinity and the Christian faith and its three colours recall the native Indians, the fertile soil, and the pure water. The ten stars stand for the ten parishes and the red disc for social justice.

The flag of the President has a dark green field with the coat of arms in the centre, crowned with a British lion. It depicts palm trees, an indigenous frog and the sea.

**THE PRESIDENT'S
FLAG**

The supporters are two sisserou parrots

The national motto is in Creole – 'Aprés Bondie C'est La Ter' meaning 'After the good Lord (we love) the soil'

St Lucia

Ratio: 1:2   Adopted: 1 March 1967   Usage: National and Civil

The blue field represents the sea

This symbol represents twin peaks of the Pitons – two famous volcanic mountains

NORTH
AMERICA

Dominica
Martinique
ST LUCIA
St Vincent &
The Grenadines   *Barbados*

St Lucia, first settled in 1605, was fought over by the French and the British, finally ceding to Britain in 1814. It became independent in 1979.

The flag was adopted when St Lucia became a British Associated State in 1967. It was designed by a local artist, Dunstan St Omer. The blue field represents the sea, from which arise the twin peaks of the Pitons said to be 'rising sheer out of the sea and looking skyward – a symbol of hope'. The yellow triangle stands for sunshine and the black arrowhead on white, for the twin cultures of the island. On independence, the flag was retained, but the height of the yellow triangle was increased.

A new form of the arms was also adopted, symbolizing the national motto: 'The Land, the People, the Light'. Apart from the Governor-General's flag and that of the capital, Castries, no other flags are known.

THE GOVERNOR-GENERAL'S STANDARD

The Royal Crest of England, with a British lion and crown

The state's title is placed on the scroll

SAINT LUCIA

St Vincent & the Grenadines

Ratio: 2:3   Adopted: *12 October 1985*   Usage: *National and Civil*

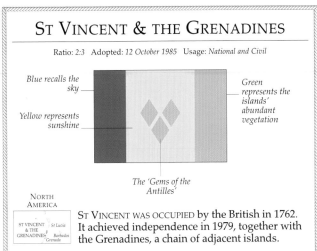

Blue recalls the sky

Yellow represents sunshine

Green represents the islands' abundant vegetation

The 'Gems of the Antilles'

NORTH AMERICA

ST VINCENT & THE GRENADINES   *St Lucia*   *Barbados*   *Grenada*

ST VINCENT WAS OCCUPIED by the British in 1762. It achieved independence in 1979, together with the Grenadines, a chain of adjacent islands.

The basic design and colours of the flag date from the flag hoisted on the day of independence in 1979. It had the arms of the islands placed on a stylized breadfruit leaf in the centre. Its blue, yellow and green stripes were derived from the common colours of the flags assigned to the Associated States by the College of Arms. The breadfruit recalled the British introduction of the breadfruit tree into the Caribbean from the South Seas.

Although this first flag was designed by a local islander, the design did not please all the people of St Vincent and the Grenadines, and, in 1985, moves were made to secure a new design.

A NEW NATIONAL FLAG
After a local competition failed to produce a satisfactory design, the problem was submitted to a Swiss graphic artist who suggested what is now the current design. In this, the 'V' formed by the diamonds stands for St Vincent, and the diamonds represent its local sobriquet the 'Gems of the Antilles'.

ARMS OF ST VINCENT
The coat of arms was first introduced in 1912. It depicts two women, one standing holding an olive branch, the other kneeling to represent peace and justice, which is the national motto – *'Pax, Justitia'*. This appears on a scroll at the base.

BARBADOS

Ratio: *2:3*   Adopted: *30 November 1966*   Usage: *National and Civil*

Blue represents the sea

The broken trident represents a break with the past

Gold reflects the golden sands of Barbados

NORTH AMERICA

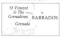

BARBADOS WAS FIRST settled by the British in 1627. It became a colony and achieved self-government in 1961 and independence in 1966.

The current flag was adopted at the time of independence. It was the winning design in a national competition, won by Grantley Prescod, a local art teacher.

THE SYMBOLISM OF THE FLAG

Prescod interpreted the stripes as representing the blue seas and the golden sands which surround the island. The trident is adapted from the previous flag-badge which depicted Britannia holding a trident (symbolic of her rule over the seas). Here the trident is without a shaft, indicating a break with the colonial past. It is also the emblem of the sea god, Neptune, and reflects the importance of the sea to Barbados.

ARMS OF BARBADOS

The coat of arms was granted by HM Queen Elizabeth II in 1966, on a visit to the island. The shield depicts a bearded fig-tree, after which the island takes its name, between two 'Pride of Barbados' flowers. The crest is an arm holding two sugarcanes in the form of a St Andrew's Cross. This commemorates independence, which was achieved on St Andrew's Day, 30 November, in 1966.

Barbados also has a Governor's standard. It is the same as that of the Governor of St Lucia (*see page 38*), except that it bears the title 'Barbados' on the scroll beneath the Royal Crest.

GRENADA

Ratio: 3:5   Adopted: 7 February 1974   Usage: National and Civil

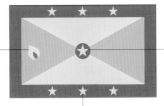

A nutmeg, Grenada's most famous product

The central star and disc represent the capital St. George's

The six outer stars stand for the six parishes

NORTH AMERICA

St Vincent & The Grenadines   Barbados
GRENADA
Venezuela   Trinidad & Tobago

FIRST SETTLED BY FRANCE, Grenada was invaded by Britain in 1762. It became an Associated State in 1967 and fully independent in 1974.

The flag used prior to independence in 1967 also featured a nutmeg, since Grenada is a major world supplier of this commodity, and is known as the 'Spice Island'.

Other features of the flag derive from the coat of arms granted on 6 December 1973, including the red, yellow and green colours.

SYMBOLISM OF THE FLAG

The yellow star on a red disc stands for the Borough of St. George's , Grenada's capital, and the other six stars for the remaining six parishes.

In the official interpretation the red stands for courage and vitality, the yellow for wisdom and warmth, and the green for vegetation and agriculture. When the flag is used at sea its proportions are altered from 3:5 to a longer form (1:2).

THE NATIONAL ARMS

The coat of arms depicts the *Santa Maria*, Columbus' ship, a lion representing national liberty and a lily emblem symbolizing the Virgin Mary. The shield is supported by two characteristic local creatures, an armadillo and a ramier pigeon. Beneath the shield is a representation of the Grand Etang lake, and, on a scroll at the base, what must be one of the world's longest national mottos: 'Ever conscious of God we aspire, build and advance as one people'.

TRINIDAD & TOBAGO

Ratio: 3:5   Adopted: *31 August 1962*   Usage: *National and Civil*

White represents the sea

Black symbolizes the strength of the people

Red stands for the people

NORTH AMERICA

TRINIDAD AND TOBAGO were separate British colonies, which united in 1889. They became independent in 1962 and a republic in 1976.

The flag adopted at independence was chosen from among designs sent in by the public. The same colours are used in the arms.

A flag for HM Queen Elizabeth II was adopted after independence, but it became obsolete following the formation of the republic.

The President has a flag of blue with the arms in the centre. The coat of arms depicts the three ships of Columbus who landed here in 1498. Beneath the ships are two golden hummingbirds. The supporters of the coat of arms are also local birds and the whole shield stands on a scene depicting waves breaking against the rocky coasts of the islands.

Trinidad also has flags for the Prime Minister and other ministers.

THE PRESIDENT'S FLAG

The top of the shield depicts two hummingbirds

The scarlet ibis is one of many local birds

The cocrico – a local bird

In 1498 Columbus discovered Trinidad and his ships appear on the shield

COLOMBIA

Ratio: 2:3   Adopted: *17 December 1819*   Usage: *National*

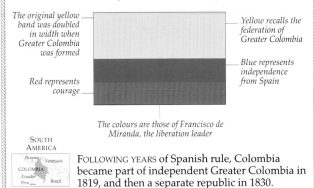

The original yellow band was doubled in width when Greater Colombia was formed

Yellow recalls the federation of Greater Colombia

Blue represents independence from Spain

Red represents courage

The colours are those of Francisco de Miranda, the liberation leader

SOUTH AMERICA

FOLLOWING YEARS of Spanish rule, Colombia became part of independent Greater Colombia in 1819, and then a separate republic in 1830.

The flag of Greater Colombia, adopted in 1819, was retained by Colombia after independence in 1930. For a while the stripes were arranged vertically, but the original version was restored in 1861.

There are two variant flags. The civil ensign has a red-bordered, blue oval bearing a white star in the centre,

used to distinguish it from the flag of Ecuador. The state flag and naval ensign have the arms in the centre.

THE NATIONAL ARMS

The coat of arms dates from 1834. It includes a pomegranate, the symbol of Granada in Spain, after which the area was once named.

ARMS OF COLOMBIA

The crest is a condor frequently used in South American heraldry

The Cap of Liberty

A map of the Isthmus of Panama

National motto – 'Libertad y Orden' meaning 'Liberty and Order'

A pomegranate recalls New Granada, Colombia's former name when a Spanish colony

VENEZUELA

Ratio: 2:3   Adopted: 20 April 1836   Usage: National and Civil

Blue represents Venezuela's independence from Spain

Stars represent the seven provinces that supported independence

Red symbolizes courage

The flag is most similar to that of liberation leader Francisco de Miranda

SOUTH AMERICA

VENEZUELA WAS once part of the Spanish province of New Granada. It then joined Greater Colombia from 1819 until independence in 1830.

The Venezuelan flag was the invention of Francisco de Miranda, who initiated the freedom of New Granada in 1806. At that time it had no stars; they were added in 1836 to symbolize the provinces that had supported the Declaration of Independence in 1811. The original plain tricolour was altered in 1819,

to make the yellow double width, for use as the flag of Greater Colombia.

After independence in 1836, the flag reverted to stripes of equal width and the stars were added.

The coat of arms dates from the 19th century but has altered frequently, especially the inscription. The present form dates from 1953.

ARMS OF VENEZUELA

The wheatsheaf represents fertility

A running horse symbolizes liberty

The arms appear in the canton of the state flag and naval ensign

Two horns of plenty symbolize abundance

The flag and weapons represent independence

The name of the state, 'Republica de Venezuela'

GUYANA

Ratio: 3:5   Adopted: *20 May 1966*   Usage: *National and Civil*

Red recalls the people's dynamism and zeal for reform

The 'Golden Arrow' represents a bright future

Yellow is symbolic of mineral wealth

Green recalls the vast forests and fields

The white and black fimbriations were added by the College of Arms

SOUTH AMERICA

GUYANA WAS ACQUIRED by the UK in 1814. It became independent in 1966 and a republic within the UK Commonwealth in 1970.

The flag is known as the 'Golden Arrow' because of the arrow-head that flies across the green field. The original design had a red field, but this was altered by the College of Arms in 1966, which also added the black and white fimbriations.

The green and yellow stand for natural resources and the red for the 'zeal and dynamism [of the inhabitants] in building the nation'.

THE PRESIDENT'S STANDARD
Adopted in 1970, it is a banner of the arms granted in 1966. It depicts a green shield in the centre charged with an Amerindian crown in gold, a Victoria lily and a native pheasant.

THE PRESIDENT'S STANDARD

The President's flag was adopted in 1970, it is a square banner of the arms

Crown of a cacique, or Amerindian chief

A Victoria Regia water lily, growing from stylized heraldic water

A native canje pheasant

SURINAM

Ratio: 2:3 Adopted: 25 November 1975 Usage: National and Civil

Green and red were the colours of the political parties at the time of independence

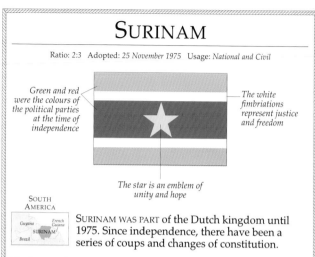

The white fimbriations represent justice and freedom

The star is an emblem of unity and hope

SOUTH AMERICA

SURINAM WAS PART of the Dutch kingdom until 1975. Since independence, there have been a series of coups and changes of constitution.

The flag was chosen in 1975 by a parliamentary commission, on the basis of designs sent in by the public. The object was to choose a flag which harmonized the colours of the main political groups (green and red) into a design suggestive of unity and progress. The star is thus the emblem of unity and hope for the future, and the white fimbriations,

separating the red and green, stand for justice and freedom.

THE PRESIDENT'S STANDARD
This has a white panel in place of the star and contains the state arms. The coat of arms dates back to the 17th century and the time of Dutch rule, but was revised in 1959 and again in 1975.

THE PRESIDENT'S STANDARD

On the shield, a ship reflects commerce, a diamond, mining, and a tree, agriculture

The supporters are Amerindians

The national motto – 'Justitia, Pietas, Fides' meaning 'Justice, Peace, Faith'

ECUADOR

Ratio: 1:2 Adopted: 26 September 1860 Usage: National

Yellow is the colour of federation

Red symbolizes courage

Blue, red and yellow are the colours of Francisco de Miranda

Blue recalls independence from Spain

SOUTH AMERICA

ECUADOR, formerly a Spanish colony, joined the state of Greater Colombia in 1822. It seceded from the federation in 1830 to form a republic.

The 1819 flag of Greater Colombia was restored in Ecuador in 1860 and since then the flags of Ecuador and Colombia have been very similar. The national arms were added to the centre of the basic civil flag in 1900, creating a distinct flag for national and state purposes. The civil flag on land and sea does not contain the arms, making it almost identical to the flag of Colombia, except for its proportions. When used abroad, the flag always contains the arms.

ARMS OF ECUADOR
The coat of arms dates from 1845 and depicts Mount Chimborazo and the mouth of the Guyas River.

ARMS OF ECUADOR

Four signs of the Zodiac represent the months from March to May

An allegorical scene depicts Mount Chimborazo, South America's highest peak

An Andean condor symbolizes bravery and liberty

A ship at the mouth of the Guyas River representing commerce

The axe and fasces are symbols of republicanism

PERU

Ratio: 2:3   Adopted: 25 February 1825   Usage: National and Civil

The colours also recall those of the Incas, who ruled much of Peru until European colonization

Red and white are the colours chosen by San Martín, 'El Liberador' (the Liberator)

SOUTH AMERICA

PERU WAS FREED from Spanish rule in 1819 by an army led by José de San Martín. Since 1824 it has been an independent unitary republic.

The colours chosen by San Martín for the Peruvian Legion were red and white, said to be the colours of the Inca Empire, and the rising sun, also dating back to the Incas. The flag assumed its present form, dropping the sun in 1825, at the behest of Simón Bolívar, another famous liberator. As is usual in former Spanish colonies, the official flag, used by the government and the armed forces, has the coat of arms in the centre.

The coat of arms dates from 1825 and depicts a cornucopia, a *chichona* tree and a llama, surrounded by state flags. The flags do not appear on the arms placed on the official flag.

ARMS OF PERU

On the coat of arms, the wreaths are substituted for national flags

A llama

A chichona tree

This is how the coat of arms appears in the centre of the official flag and ensign

A cornucopia symbolizing prosperity

BRAZIL

Ratio: 7:10   Adopted: 15 November 1889   Usage: National and Civil

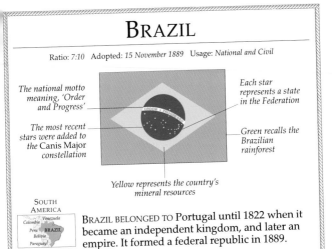

The national motto meaning, 'Order and Progress'

The most recent stars were added to the Canis Major constellation

Each star represents a state in the Federation

Green recalls the Brazilian rainforest

Yellow represents the country's mineral resources

SOUTH AMERICA

BRAZIL BELONGED TO Portugal until 1822 when it became an independent kingdom, and later an empire. It formed a federal republic in 1889.

The green field and yellow lozenge were part of the flag adopted in 1822 when independence was first achieved and the empire was declared. In 1889, the imperial arms were replaced by a view of the night sky as it appeared over Rio de Janeiro when the republic was formed. Each of the stars in the constellation represents a state of the Federation, including the Federal District. These have been altered from time to time, most recently in 1992 when the number of stars increased to 27.

THE CONSTELLATIONS

The constellations on the flag are represented in a realistic manner,

with stars of varying sizes, although the size of star does not reflect the importance of the state. In 1992, new stars were added to the constellation of *Canis Major* in the lower left section of the sky. The country's national motto, 'Ordem e Progresso' meaning, 'Order and Progress' appears on a band across the centre of the night sky.

THE NATIONAL CAPITAL

In Brasília, the capital since 1960, stands one of the world's tallest flagpoles, on which flies an enormous national flag.

Brazil also has flags for the President, the Ministry of Marine and a naval Jack.

Brazil – State flags

MANY OF THE FLAGS recall historical events, or the formation of the federal republic. The date of accession is given below the state name.

THE FEDERAL DISTRICT
1960

The flag of the Federal District dates from 1969. The green rectangle contains four arrows representing the balance of centralization and devolution in Brazil.

ACRE
1962

Adopted by the republic declared in 1899, when Acre was still part of Bolivia, the flag was retained by the state and the star was added to recall its joining the Federation.

ALAGOAS
1889

Based on the flag of 1894, this new version was instituted in 1963. In the centre is the arms, also originally dating back to 1894. It recalls various aspects of the state's industry.

AMAPÁ
1989

The flag was adopted in 1984 for the territory and retained for the state. It uses all the national colours, together with an outline of the fortress of Macapá, the state capital.

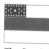

AMAZONAS
1889

The flag dates from the local uprising of 1897. The stars stand for the 25 municipalities, with the large one for Manaus, the state capital. The flag was regularized in 1982.

BAHIA
1889

The flag dates back to the uprisings of 1789 and 1798, which are recalled by the white triangle. The flag in this form was first adopted in 1889, when Bahia joined the Federation.

CEARÁ
1889

The flag was instituted in 1922 and is very similar to the national flag. The arms depicts an allegorical landscape surrounded by stars. It dates from 1897 and was revised in 1967.

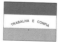

ESPÍRITO SANTO
1889

The flag was created in 1947. The Portuguese motto meaning – 'Work and Trust' – is that of the Jesuits, and the pink and blue represent the local evening sky.

Brazil – State flags

GOIÁS
1889

The flag is based on those promoted for the republic in 1889. This version has five stars for the Southern Cross similar to those in the national arms.

MARANHÃO
1889

The flag, adopted in 1889, features the star, which represents the state on the national flag, while the stripes stand for its ethnic mix.

MATO GROSSO
1889

The flag is based on the national flag, but with local interpretations of the colour arrangement and one star for the state. It was adopted in 1890.

MATO GROSSO DO SUL
1977

The design emerged from a competition held in 1978, after the new state was formed. The flag was instituted in 1979.

MINAS GERAIS
1889

The flag contains a Masonic triangle of the *Inconfidência Mineira* (miners revolt) of 1789, standing for equality.

PARÁ
1889

Based on a republican flag, it dates from 1898. The star is taken from the one for Pará on the national flag.

PARAÍBA
1889

The flag recalls Vargas' revolution in 1930. *Nego* ('I deny it') refers to the assassination of the state president.

PARANÁ
1889

The flag contains an emblem like the national flag, bearing the Southern Cross and name of the state.

PERNAMBUCO
1889

This is the flag of the Pernambuco revolution of 1817, which later became the flag of the state when the events of 1817 were celebrated.

PIAUÍ
1889

Based on the colours of the national flag, in this instance it only has one star representing the state of Piauí. It was adopted in 1922.

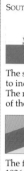

RIO DE JANEIRO
1975

The state was reconstituted in 1975 to include the state of Guanabara. The new state took over the emblems of the former state of Rio de Janeiro.

RIO GRANDE DO SUL
1889

The flag dates from the revolution of 1836, which created the Republic of Rio Grande do Sul. It was re-adopted in 1891 and the arms were added.

RORAIMA
1989

The flag, adopted when the territory became a federal state, uses the national colours and star, with a red line representing the Equator.

SÃO PAULO
1889

The flag was created in 1888 at the start of the republican revolution, and revived in 1932, with 13 stripes.

TOCANTINS
1989

After achieving statehood, a flag and arms were adopted, using blue and white from the national colours.

RIO GRANDE DO NORTE
1889

Dating from 1957, the flag uses the arms granted in 1909, thus making it one of the newest flags of the original states.

RONDÔNIA
1981

Rondônia's flag uses the four national colours and a single star symbol. It was adopted in 1981 after a design competition.

SANTA CATARINA
1889

The red and white flag precedes the republic. It was most recently regularized in 1953, when the arms were placed in the centre.

SERGIPE
1889

The flag was created in the late 19th century and adopted in 1920. In 1951 the stars were repositioned.

CHILE

Ratio: 2:3   Adopted: *18 October 1817*   Usage: *National and Civil*

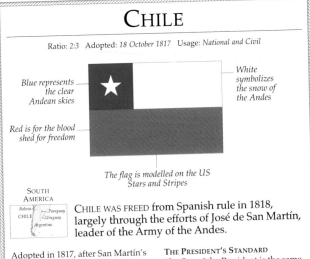

Blue represents the clear Andean skies

White symbolizes the snow of the Andes

Red is for the blood shed for freedom

The flag is modelled on the US Stars and Stripes

SOUTH AMERICA

CHILE WAS FREED from Spanish rule in 1818, largely through the efforts of José de San Martín, leader of the Army of the Andes.

Adopted in 1817, after San Martín's victory at Chacabuco, the national flag of Chile was preceded by at least two other versions during the early years of separatism. The current flag was based on the Stars and Stripes.

The white star was reserved for use only on the official flag until 1864, when the starred flag was made official for all purposes.

THE PRESIDENT'S STANDARD
The flag of the President is the same as the national flag, with the national arms in the centre. The coat of arms dates from 1834. It is supported by an *huemal* deer and a condor. The crest is formed from the feathers of the *rhea* bird. The motto – '*Por La Razon o La Fuerza*' means 'By reason or by force.'

THE PRESIDENT'S STANDARD

A crest of feathers from the rhea bird

An huemal deer, of the high Andes

The condor is a common symbol on South American arms

BOLIVIA

Ratio: 2:3   Adopted: 30 November 1851   Usage: National and Civil

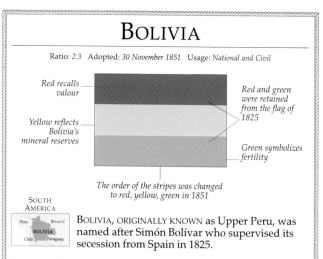

Red recalls valour

Red and green were retained from the flag of 1825

Yellow reflects Bolivia's mineral reserves

Green symbolizes fertility

The order of the stripes was changed to red, yellow, green in 1851

SOUTH AMERICA

BOLIVIA, ORIGINALLY KNOWN as Upper Peru, was named after Simón Bolívar who supervised its secession from Spain in 1825.

The flag of 1825 had three stripes of red-green-red, with five gold stars within laurel wreaths. These stood for the original five departments.

A NEW TRICOLOUR

In 1826, the flag was altered to three equal stripes of yellow, green and red with the arms in the centre.

It was last altered in 1851, when the order of the stripes was changed to red, yellow, green.

The official flag still has the arms in the centre. It was regulated in 1888 and depicts Mount Potosí, an alpaca, a wheatsheaf and a breadfruit tree. The oval ring contains nine stars for the nine departments.

ARMS OF BOLIVIA

As on many South American arms, the crest is a condor

The allegorical scene on the shield represents Bolivia's agricultural and industrial wealth

The flags and weapons represent the people's willingness to defend the state

The nine stars represent Bolivia's nine departments

PARAGUAY

Ratio: 3:5 Adopted: 25 November 1842 Usage: National and Civil

On the reverse, the flag is charged with the Treasury Seal

The Star of May is used as a symbol of freedom on many South American flags

The colours were influenced by the French Tricolore, which had become a symbol of liberation

SOUTH AMERICA

PARAGUAY DECLARED its independence from Spain in 1811 and has remained an independent republic ever since.

The colours of the flag and the Star of May emblem date from the Declaration of Independence. A number of variant designs existed prior to the current design, which was regularized in 1842. The current flag has a separate emblem on each side, a practice dating from the time of José de Francia, in power from 1814–40. During his regime one side of the flag carried the arms of Spain and the other the arms of Asunción.

The current emblems, adopted in 1821, but not officially sanctioned until 1842, are the national arms on the front (obverse) and the Treasury Seal on the back (reverse).

STATE ARMS ON THE OBVERSE

TREASURY SEAL ON THE REVERSE

Name of the state

The Star of May recalls the date of independence

The Cap of Liberty guarded by a lion

The state motto – 'Paz y Justicia' ('Peace and Justice')

URUGUAY

Ratio: 2:3 Adopted: *11 July 1830* Usage: *National and Civil*

The Sun of May has been a national emblem since the 19th century

Blue and white are also the national colours of Argentina, from which this flag derives

The nine stripes represent the nine departments

SOUTH AMERICA

HISTORICALLY A SPANISH colony, Uruguay was annexed to Brazil and then to Argentina before becoming fully independent in 1830.

The colours, blue and white, and the Sun of May on the current flag come from the Argentinian flag.

THE FLAG OF ARTIGAS
The colours were brought to Uruguay by José Artigas, who led the movement for separation. His flag was blue and white striped, with a red diagonal. Variations of this flag remained in use after Uruguay was annexed to Brazil in 1821.

When full independence was assumed, the present form of the flag was instituted. The nine stripes represent the nine departments. The Sun of May has been used as the national emblem since 1815 and now appears as the crest on the coat of arms.

FLAG OF ARTIGAS

The colours derived from those of Argentina's flag

This flag is now used as a Jack for naval vessels

Red represents the 'Banda Oriental' (the 'East Bank') of Uruguay

ARGENTINA

Ratio: 1:2   Adopted: 12 February 1812   Usage: National and Civil

Blue and white were formed into a flag by Manuel Belgrano, the leader of the revolution

The Sun of May was added in 1818 to create a flag for state use

Blue and white recall the sky when the first uprising for independence was staged

SOUTH AMERICA

ARGENTINA ACHIEVED its independence from Spain in 1816. Liberation demonstrations began in Buenos Aires on 25 May 1810.

The colours, adopted by Manuel Belgrano, the leader of the revolution, were first used at the Battle of Rosario in 1812. They were based on the blue and white cockades adopted after the 25 May gathering when, it is said, white clouds parted to reveal the blue sky and the shining sun, inspiring the 'Sun of May' emblem.

THE SUN FLAG
In 1818 the emblem and the colours were combined to form the sun flag used today as the national and official flag. The form of the sun is taken from the one depicted on the 8-*real* and 8-*escudo* coins of 1813.

The arms also used the Sun of May emblem and the national colours.

ARMS OF ARGENTINA

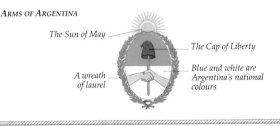

The Sun of May

The Cap of Liberty

A wreath of laurel

Blue and white are Argentina's national colours

Morocco

Ratio: *2:3*   Adopted: *17 November 1915*   Usage: *National and Civil*

Red represents the descendants of the Prophet Muhammad

The Seal of Solomon was added in 1915

AFRICA

MOROCCO HAS BEEN **independent since 1956, becoming a kingdom in 1957. The state is now ruled by the Filali Dynasty.**

Red has considerable historic significance in Morocco, proclaiming the descent of the royal family from the Prophet Muhammad via Fatima, the wife of Ali, the fourth Caliph. Red is also the colour that was used by the Sherifs of Mecca and the Imams of Yemen.

THE SEAL OF SOLOMON

From the 17th century, when Morocco was ruled by the Hassani Dynasty, the flags of the country were plain red. In 1915, during the reign of Mulay Yusuf, the green 'Seal of Solomon' was added to the national flag. The Seal is an interlaced pentangle, used as a symbol in occult law for centuries.

THE COLONIAL ERA

While Morocco was under French and Spanish control, the red flag with the seal in the centre remained in use but only inland, its use at sea was prohibited. When independence was restored in 1956 it once again became the national flag.

THE NATIONAL ARMS

After independence in 1958, Morocco adopted a national coat of arms. This depicts the sun rising over the Atlas Mountains. The arms also includes the Seal of Solomon from the national flag. On the scroll is an inscription from the Qur'an (Koran), which reads 'If you assist God, he will assist you'.

ALGERIA

Ratio: 2:3   Adopted: 3 July 1962   Usage: National and Civil

Green is the colour of Islam

White is symbolic of purity

The crescent and star of Islam recall Ottoman rule

The horns stand for good fortune and happiness

Red represents liberty

AFRICA

ALGERIA WAS occupied by the French from 1830. Independence was achieved in 1962 after a long struggle led by the National Liberation Front.

The flag of Algeria was adopted by the National Liberation Front (*Front de Libération National*) in 1954, on the basis of an older design, created in 1928, by the nationalist leader Messali Hadj. From 1958–62 it was the flag of the Provisional Government in exile, but it was retained when independence was achieved in 1962 and has remained unchanged ever since.

SYMBOLISM IN THE FLAG
The green in the hoist is the traditional colour of Islam and the white represents purity. The horns of the crescent are longer than usual and represent increase or good fortune and happiness, whilst the whole emblem recalls the period of Ottoman rule during the 16th century and its colour, red, is symbolic of liberty.

THE NAVAL ENSIGN
The naval ensign has two crossed anchors in the canton. This device is used on the naval ensigns of several Arab countries, following the example of Egypt.

THE EMBLEM OF ALGERIA
The state coat of arms is based on the well-known local emblem of the 'Hand of Fatima'. It also contains the crescent and star of Islam, alongside symbols reflecting both agriculture and industry.

TUNISIA

Ratio: 2:3   Adopted: *1835*   Usage: *National and Civil*

The crescent and star of Islam —

— *Red taken from the flag of Turkey*

PART OF THE TURKISH EMPIRE until 1881, Tunisia then became a French Protectorate. In 1957, it became a republic when the 'Bey' was deposed.

The flag is based on that of the Turkish Empire and was adopted by the 'Bey', the hereditary ruler of Tunisia, in 1835, primarily as a military flag. During the French administration (1881–1957) it became a sea flag, with the French *Tricolore* in the canton; this was removed when independence was achieved in 1956.

The coat of arms of Tunisia has been altered since the abolition of the monarchy, most recently in 1963, and unusually has the motto on a scroll actually on the shield. The motto reads – in Arabic – 'Order, Liberty, Justice'. The ship, lion and balance were retained from the previous arms.

ARMS OF TUNISIA

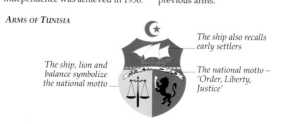

The ship also recalls early settlers

The ship, lion and balance symbolize the national motto

The national motto – 'Order, Liberty, Justice'

LIBYA

Ratio: 3:5 Adopted: 1977 Usage: *National and Civil*

Green is the
national colour
of Libya

It is the only
national flag
of a single
plain colour

Green also reflects the
people's devotion to Islam

AFRICA

LIBYA ACHIEVED independence in 1951, but in 1969
the King was deposed and Libya formed a
republic led by Colonel Gadaffi.

The flag of the independent
kingdom was red, black and green
with a crescent and star in the
centre, but after the revolution of
1969, the flag became three simple
stripes of red, white and black.

In 1971, Libya joined the Federation
of Arab Republics with Egypt and
Syria which used a similar flag with

a hawk emblem in the centre and the
name of the country beneath it.

When Libya quit the Federation in
1977, the new plain green flag was
adopted. The national emblem
remains similar to the one used
while Libya was part of the
Federation, which shows the
Hawk of Quraish.

ARMS OF LIBYA

The Hawk of Quraish is
the emblem of the tribe
of Muhammad

The title of the
state – 'The
Great Socialist
People's Libyan
Arab Republic'

EGYPT

Ratio: 2:3   Adopted: *4 October 1984*   Usage: *National and Civil*

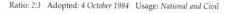

Red, white
and black are
pan-Arab
colours

Eagle of
Saladin

AFRICA

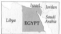

EGYPT WAS A KINGDOM until 1953. From 1958–1961 it joined the United Arab Republic and from 1972–1977 the Federation of Arab Republics.

As a kingdom, the flag was green with a white crescent and three stars.

THE UNITED ARAB REPUBLIC
When the United Arab Republic (UAR) was formed in 1958, they adapted the flag of the Liberation Rally which led the independence revolt of 1952–53. The UAR flag was red, white and black, with two green stars in the centre of the white stripe. In 1972, when the Federation was formed, the stars were replaced with the Hawk of the Quraish *(see page 61)*, in gold, above the state name.

In 1984, Egypt reverted to the gold eagle used by the Liberation Rally. These colours and the eagle emblem have been widely copied in other Arab countries.

*FLAG OF THE
LIBERATION RALLY
1952–58*

The gold eagle is said to be the Eagle of Saladin

The crescent and stars were retained from the old national flag

SUDAN

Ratio: 1:2   Adopted: 20 May 1970   Usage: National and Civil

Red represents socialism

Green is the colour of Islam and prosperity

Red, white, black and green are pan-Arab colours

White represents purity and optimism

AFRICA

RULED JOINTLY by Egypt and Britain from 1877, Sudan became independent in 1956. Since then it has had a series of different regimes.

The flag used at independence was a horizontal tricolour of blue, yellow and green, but following the formation of the Democratic Republic in 1968, a new flag was chosen by competition.

A PAN-ARAB FLAG
This is very similar to the flags of other Arab countries, with the green

as a triangle in the hoist. White is believed to represent purity and optimism, red stands for socialism and green for prosperity.

In 1969 a new arms was adopted, with a secretary bird bearing a shield from the time of the Mahdi, (who briefly ruled Sudan in the 19th century). Two scrolls are placed above and below the secretary bird.

ARMS OF SUDAN

The national motto – 'Al-nasr lina' ('Victory is ours')

A secretary bird bears the shield

The title of the state – 'Al-Jamhuriya as-Sudaniya' ('Republic of Sudan')

ERITREA

Ratio: 2:3 Adopted: *24 May 1993* Usage: *National and Civil*

An olive branch is encircled by a wreath representing Eritrean autonomy

Green, blue and red are the colours of the Eritrean People's Liberation Front

AFRICA

ERITREA WAS FEDERATED to Ethiopia in 1952 and fully integrated in 1962. From 1972, a long war of secession led to independence in 1993.

The flag of the Eritrean People's Liberation Front (EPLF), which campaigned for independence, is green and blue with a red triangle bearing a gold star. The flag adopted on independence retained the colours and pattern, but replaced the star with the emblem used previously for autonomous Eritrea. This is an olive branch surrounded by a wreath of olive leaves. Originally this emblem was green on a blue flag, but it is now yellow.

THE PRESIDENT'S FLAG

The President's flag contains the national arms, which depicts a camel in a desert, with the name of the state underneath in English, Tigrinya and Arabic.

THE PRESIDENT'S FLAG

The arms of Eritrea

The arms is surrounded by a wreath of leaves

The colours of the national flag are used

DJIBOUTI

Ratio: 21:38 Adopted: 27 June 1977 Usage: National and Civil

Light blue represents the Issa people

White, green and light blue are the colours of the LPAI

The star represents the unity of the state

Green represents the Afar people, with their land and links to Islam

ONCE KNOWN AS FRENCH SOMALILAND, and from 1967 as the Territory of the Afars and Issas, Djibouti gained independence in 1977.

The national flag adopted in 1977 was an adaptation of the flag of the *Ligue Populaire Africaine pour l'Indépendance* (LPAI) which led Djibouti to independence. The LPAI flag had a red triangle with a white star. For the national flag, adopted at independence, the star was placed in an upright, rather than a slanted position, and the proportions of the flag were lengthened. The colours stand for the Issas and the Afars, the two peoples of Djibouti at independence, and the red star for the unity of the diverse state.

The coat of arms is centred around a local Somali shield and spear, bordered by two hunting knives.

ARMS OF DJIBOUTI

A Somali shield and weapons; two hunting knives and a spear

The red star is a traditional symbol of unity

The coat of arms contains a local shield

ETHIOPIA

Ratio: 1:2   Adopted: 6 February 1996   Usage: National and Civil

The emblem represents diversity and unity

Yellow is the colour of peace and love

Green recalls the land and hope for the future

The colours date back to the 19th century

Red is symbolic of strength

AFRICA

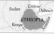

ETHIOPIA WAS RECOGNIZED as an empire in the 19th century. It was occupied by Italy from 1936–41. The Emperor was overthrown in 1974.

The three traditional colours: green, yellow and red, date back to the Emperor Menelik (1889–1913) and were first used in a flag in 1895.

The current flag and emblem were adopted after the defeat of the Marxist Mengistu regime, in power from 1974–1991. The emblem is intended to represent both the diversity and unity of the country.

EMBLEM OF ETHIOPIA

ETHIOPIA AND THE RASTAFARI
In the 1930s the Ethiopian colours became popular with black activists in Jamaica who looked to Ethiopia for political and spiritual guidance. Since then, these colours (along with black from the flag of Marcus Garvey [see page 7]) have become linked with the Rastafarian movement, and have spread to other African countries.

Blue represents peace

The sun's rays symbolize prosperity

The star represents diversity and unity

SOMALIA

Ratio: 2:3   Adopted: 12 October 1954   Usage: National and Civil

The five-pointed star represents the branches of the Somali race; in Ethiopia, Kenya, Djibouti and the former British and Italian colonies

The blue is the same as that used by the United Nations

The star of unity

AFRICA

MODERN SOMALIA is a combination of the former Italian territory and British Somaliland. Since 1991 it has been in a state of civil war.

The flag was adopted by the Italian Trusteeship Territory in 1954 on the basis of the blue and white flag of the United Nations, which was supervising the territory at the time. It was retained when Somalia became independent in 1960. The five-pointed star is said to stand for the five branches of the Somali race including those living in Ethiopia, Djibouti and Kenya.

ARMS OF SOMALIA

The coat of arms was adopted in 1956. The leopards which support the shield and the white star were also found on the arms used during the Italian administration.

ARMS OF SOMALIA

The shield is based on the national flag

The supporters are leopards; a leopard also featured on the shield of the colonial arms

Below the shield are two palm branches and two spears

UGANDA

Ratio: 2:3 Adopted: *9 October 1962* Usage: *National and Civil*

The colours of the flag represent the Ugandan people, sunlight and brotherhood

The great crested crane is the national badge of Uganda

Black, yellow and red are the party colours of the UPC

AFRICA

SINCE INDEPENDENCE in 1962, Uganda has suffered years of upheaval. Under the current regime some stability has been restored.

The dominant party at the time of independence was the Uganda People's Congress (UPC), and the new national flag was an adaptation of its tricolour with the addition of the crane badge in the centre. This dates back to before independence when the colonial badge of Uganda was the great crested crane. It also appears as one of the supporters on

Uganda's coat of arms granted on 3 September 1962. The arms depicts a local shield, in an allegorical landscape with tea and cotton plants.

THE PRESIDENT'S STANDARD

The flag for the President was adopted in 1963 and consists of the arms on a red field with the national colours along the lower edge.

THE PRESIDENT'S STANDARD

A deer is one of the supporters

Tea and cotton are Uganda's most important crops

A great crested crane supports the shield

Blue and white represent the waters of the Nile and of Lake Victoria

KENYA

Ratio: 2:3 Adopted: *12 December 1963* Usage: *National and Civil*

Black, red and green are KANU party colours

The white fimbriations were added to the KANU flag to create the national flag

White was added to represent the democratic party

The African shield is also used in the national arms

AFRICA

KENYA BECAME a colony in 1920 having previously been known as British East Africa. It became independent in 1963 and a republic in 1964.

The flag adopted at independence was based on that of the Kenya Africa National Union (KANU); the dominant political party. For the national flag, white fimbriations were added, and the shield and spears were re-drawn.

A coat of arms was adopted in 1963 which makes use of the same shield and spears, but with a white cock in the centre, grasping an axe.

Kenya was the first African country to use a shield of traditional design in its coat of arms, a practice which has since been followed in many other new states. It was also the first to give the motto in a local language, in this case Swahili.

ARMS OF KENYA

The shield stands on a representation of Mount Kenya

The cock with an axe is the KANU party symbol

'Harambee' meaning 'Pull Together' in Swahili

HARAMBEE

69

RWANDA

Ratio: 2:3   Adopted: *September 1961*   Usage: *National and Civil*

'R' stands for Rwanda

Red, yellow and green are pan-African colours

RWANDA, originally part of German East Africa, was taken over by Belgium after the First World War. It became independent on 1 July 1962.

On the original flag adopted by Rwanda, the stripes were ordered green, yellow and red. However, before Independence Day, Mali assumed a flag like this, and a new version had to be found. The solution chosen was to alter the order of the colours and to add the country's initial in the centre.

Rwanda is one of many countries in Africa which uses an adaptation of the colours of Ethiopia for its flag. Despite the upheavals of modern times neither the flag nor the emblem have been altered.

The arms depicts weapons, tools and the national motto on a shield, surmounted by a dove of peace.

ARMS OF RWANDA

National flags

A hoe

The bow and arrow are traditional weapons

The dove of peace

A pruning knife and hoe represent agriculture

The national motto – 'Liberté-Cooperation-Progrès' ('Freedom, Co-operation, Progress')

BURUNDI

Ratio: 2:3   Adopted: *28 June 1967*   Usage: *National and Civil*

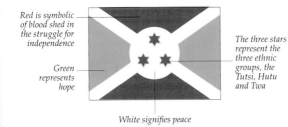

Red is symbolic of blood shed in the struggle for independence

The three stars represent the three ethnic groups, the Tutsi, Hutu and Twa

Green represents hope

White signifies peace

LIKE RWANDA, Burundi was a German, then a Belgian territory. It achieved independence as a kingdom in 1962 and became a republic in 1966.

The flag adopted at independence had a drum – symbolic of the monarchy – and a sorghum plant in the central disc. When the kingdom was abolished the drum was removed, and a year later the sorghum plant was replaced by the three stars, said to symbolize the main ethnic groups.

THE NATIONAL ARMS

The coat of arms has also been altered. The royal drum which was above the shield was removed, a more republican motto was adopted, and the four spears were reduced to three, again to represent the ethnic groups. The golden lion's face also featured on the royal badge.

ARMS OF BURUNDI

Three spears represent Burundi's ethnic groups

The lion's face has remained unchanged since the original arms were adopted in 1962

The motto is 'Unite-Travail-Progres' meaning 'Unity, Work, Progress'

CENTRAL AFRICAN REPUBLIC

Ratio: 2:3   Adopted: 1 December 1958   Usage: National and Civil

The star represents hope of a union under France

Red, white and blue are taken from the French Tricolore

Red, yellow and green are pan-African colours

The vertical stripe represents unity and the blood of humanity

AFRICA

PREVIOUSLY KNOWN AS Ubangui-Shari, the Central African Republic was formed as an autonomous state in 1958 under French protection.

The flag is unique in that it combines the pan-African colours with those of France, the former colonial power. This was done in the hope that neighbouring states would join a federation under French protection, but this never materialized; the star represents the hope of achieving this goal. The state became an empire under the Emperor Bokassa from 1976–79, but no change was made to the national symbols.

The coat of arms is intended to symbolize both the Central African Republic and its important position in the centre of Africa. The upper scroll bears the motto of the former ruling party; it means 'A Man is a Man'.

ARMS OF THE CENTRAL AFRICAN REPUBLIC

An elephant and a baobab tree

The national motto – 'Unité, Dignité, Travail' meaning 'Unity, Dignity, Work'

The central feature is a gold star on a map of Africa, symbolizing the position of the Central African Republic

The hand was the party emblem of the dominant party in 1963, when the arms was adopted

CONGO (ZAIRE)

Ratio: 2:3 Adopted: *17 May 1997* Usage: *National and Civil*

The six stars represent the six original provinces of Congo (Zaire) in 1960

The flag was flown by Kabila's forces, during their struggle for control of the country

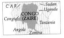

CONGO (ZAIRE) was formerly the Belgian Congo and the Congo Free State. It gained independence in 1960, but has yet to achieve political stability.

The current flag of Congo (Zaire) was re-adopted on the 17 May 1997, following a successful *coup d'etat* by rebel forces.

THE MPR FLAG
Prior to the coup, the flag of Zaire was based on the party flag of the *Movement Populaire de la Révolution* (MPR) which came to power in 1971.

THE FLAGS OF 1960–1971
The current flag was first adopted at independence from Belgium in 1960. In 1963, it was replaced by a blue flag with a single yellow star in the canton and a yellow-bordered, red stripe running diagonally. It is believed that the new leader of Congo (Zaire), Laurent Kabila, may revert to the flag of 1963.

CONGO-KINSHASA 1963–1971

It is not yet known whether this flag will become the national flag of Congo (Zaire)

This flag was adopted on 1 July 1963, it was the national flag until 1971.

NIGER

Ratio: 2:3   Adopted: 23 November 1959   Usage: National and Civil

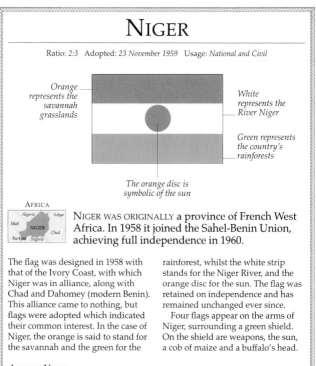

Orange represents the savannah grasslands

White represents the River Niger

Green represents the country's rainforests

The orange disc is symbolic of the sun

AFRICA

NIGER WAS ORIGINALLY a province of French West Africa. In 1958 it joined the Sahel-Benin Union, achieving full independence in 1960.

The flag was designed in 1958 with that of the Ivory Coast, with which Niger was in alliance, along with Chad and Dahomey (modern Benin). This alliance came to nothing, but flags were adopted which indicated their common interest. In the case of Niger, the orange is said to stand for the savannah and the green for the rainforest, whilst the white strip stands for the Niger River, and the orange disc for the sun. The flag was retained on independence and has remained unchanged ever since.

Four flags appear on the arms of Niger, surrounding a green shield. On the shield are weapons, the sun, a cob of maize and a buffalo's head.

ARMS OF NIGER

Weapons represent military achievements

The title of the state – in French – is placed on the scroll

Maize represents the country's agriculture

The buffalo's head reflects pastoral farming

REPUBLIQUE   DU NIGER

CHAD

Ratio: 2:3   Adopted: 6 November 1959   Usage: National and Civil

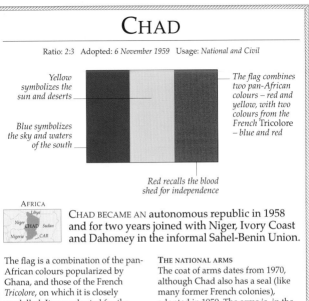

Yellow symbolizes the sun and deserts

Blue symbolizes the sky and waters of the south

The flag combines two pan-African colours – red and yellow, with two colours from the French Tricolore – blue and red

Red recalls the blood shed for independence

AFRICA

CHAD BECAME AN **autonomous republic in 1958 and for two years joined with Niger, Ivory Coast and Dahomey in the informal Sahel-Benin Union.**

The flag is a combination of the pan-African colours popularized by Ghana, and those of the French *Tricolore*, on which it is closely modelled. It was adopted for the autonomous republic and retained on independence in 1960. Despite many upheavals since independence the flag has not been changed.

THE NATIONAL ARMS

The coat of arms dates from 1970, although Chad also has a seal (like many former French colonies), adopted in 1959. The arms is. in the colours of the national flag and is supported by a lion and a wild goat. The medal below the shield is the badge of the National Order of Chad.

ARMS OF CHAD

The red symbol is for salt, the country's main mineral

A mountain goat represents the north of Chad

The wavy bars symbolize Lake Chad

The lion is symbolic of the south of the country

The national motto – 'Unite, Travail, Progres' ('Unity, Work, Progress')

MAURITANIA

Ratio: 2:3 Adopted: *1 April 1959* Usage: *National and Civil*

Green also recalls the country's Islamic faith

The crescent and star of Islam

Yellow and green are both pan-African colours

AFRICA

Western Sahara *Algeria*
MAURITANIA *Mali*
Senegal

MAURITANIA BECAME fully independent from France in 1960. From 1976–79 it occupied part of Western Sahara; now occupied by Morocco.

The flag was adopted in 1959 for the autonomous republic. It consists simply of a yellow crescent and star of Islam on a green field, expressive of the country's full title – 'The Mauritanian Islamic Republic'.

Mauritania also has seal, like those used in many former French colonies. It is uncoloured and

represents a real seal, used for certifying documents.

It bears the title of the state around the edge. In the centre are the Islamic crescent and star emblems. These are decorated with a palm branch and a millet plant, both important national plants. The seal was adopted for Mauritania in 1960.

SEAL OF MAURITANIA

The star and crescent of Islam

The name of the country is given in both French and Arabic

A millet plant

A palm branch

MALI

Ratio: 2:3   Adopted: *1 March 1961*   Usage: *National and Civil*

Green, yellow and red are pan-African colours

The style of the flag is modelled on the French Tricolore

AFRICA

MALI ACHIEVED INDEPENDENCE from France in confederation with Senegal on 20 June 1960, but split away later the same year to form a republic.

The flag adopted in 1959 for the Confederation was an imitation of the flag of Ghana, but following the style of the French *Tricolore*. It was charged with a black emblem known as a *kanaga*, a stylized human figure. The colours were intended to reflect a unity with other African nations.

After the two countries split up in

1960, the flag was kept for use in Mali until 1 March 1961, when the black figure was dropped.

Mali also has a seal, like those of other former French colonies. It is uncoloured and displays a local fortress between two bows and arrows. Above the fortress is a dove of peace and below it is a rising sun.

SEAL OF MALI

The title of the state

A local fortress

A bow and arrow

The dove of peace

The national motto – 'Un Peuple, Un But, Une Foi' *meaning* 'One People, One Goal, One Faith'

SENEGAL

Ratio: 2:3   Adopted: *September 1960*   Usage: *National and Civil*

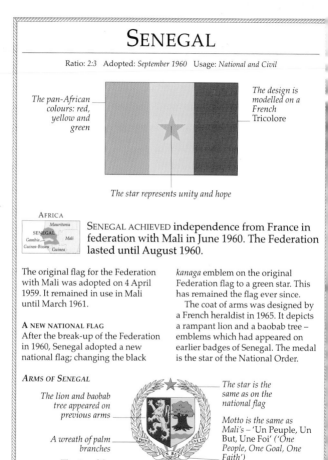

The pan-African colours: red, yellow and green

The design is modelled on a French Tricolore

The star represents unity and hope

AFRICA

SENEGAL ACHIEVED **independence from France in federation with Mali in June 1960. The Federation lasted until August 1960.**

The original flag for the Federation with Mali was adopted on 4 April 1959. It remained in use in Mali until March 1961.

A NEW NATIONAL FLAG
After the break-up of the Federation in 1960, Senegal adopted a new national flag; changing the black *kanaga* emblem on the original Federation flag to a green star. This has remained the flag ever since.

The coat of arms was designed by a French heraldist in 1965. It depicts a rampant lion and a baobab tree – emblems which had appeared on earlier badges of Senegal. The medal is the star of the National Order.

ARMS OF SENEGAL

The lion and baobab tree appeared on previous arms

A wreath of palm branches

The star of the National Order

The star is the same as on the national flag

Motto is the same as Mali's – 'Un Peuple, Un But, Une Foi' ('One People, One Goal, One Faith')

THE GAMBIA

Ratio: 2:3   Adopted: *18 February 1965*   Usage: *National and Civil*

Red represents the savannah grasslands

The blue stripe symbolizes the River Gambia

Green symbolizes the forests

AFRICA

THE GAMBIA BECAME self-governing in 1963 and fully independent of Britain on 18 February 1965. It became a republic on 24 April 1970.

The flag of the Gambia has no political basis. The blue stripe of the flag is said to represent the River Gambia flowing between the green forest and the red savannah. It was adopted at independence in 1965.

The coat of arms was granted before independence, in 1964. It makes no reference to the previous colonial badge of the Gambia and follows traditional heraldry. The two tools represent the main ethnic groups – the Mandinka and the Fulani – and the crest, above the helmet, is a local oil palm.

The federation formed with Senegal from 1981–1989 had no effect on the national symbols.

ARMS OF THE GAMBIA

The supporters are two lions, shown holding tools

The national motto – 'Progress, Peace, Prosperity'

A crest of oil palm leaves

An axe and a hoe represent the Mandinka and the Fulani, the two main ethnic groups in the Gambia

CAPE VERDE

Ratio: *10:17*　Adopted: *25 February 1992*　Usage: *National and Civil*

The ten stars stand for the ten islands of Cape Verde

The red stripe between the white represents the road to progress

Blue represents the Atlantic Ocean

CAPE VERDE WAS originally an overseas province of Portugal. It obtained independence in 1975. In 1992 a multiparty constitution was adopted.

The flag adopted in 1975 was very similar to that of Guinea-Bissau, both were based on the flag of the same dominant political party.

The current flag adopted by the new government in 1992, depicts the ocean in blue, with the islands as a ring of stars on a line of red fimbriated in white, representing the road to progress. The stars may be derived from the arms of Praia, the capital.

The national arms depicts a torch on a triangle, symbolizing unity and freedom. It also includes the ring of stars and a plumb-bob signifying rectitude and virtue, which are the 'keystones' of the Constitution.

ARMS OF CAPE VERDE

The title of the state

The stars represent the main islands of Cape Verde

The plumb-bob is symbolic of rectitude and virtue

The torch and triangle represent unity and freedom

GUINEA-BISSAU

Ratio: *1:2* Adopted: *24 September 1973* Usage: *National and Civil*

The black star represents the unity of Africa

Yellow stands for the sun

Green represents hope

Red stands for the blood shed during the struggle for independence

AFRICA

GUINEA-BISSAU is so-called to distinguish it from the former French Guinea. Formerly a territory of Portugal, it achieved self-government in 1973.

Like the former flag of Cape Verde, the flag is based on that of the *Partido Africano para a Independencia da Guiné e Cabo Verde* (PAIGC), still the dominant party in Guinea-Bissau.

THE GHANAIAN INFLUENCE
The party flag was derived from that of Ghana, which first used the pan-

African combination of red, yellow, green and black in 1957. In the Ghanaian view, the black star stands for the unity of Africa. The colours are now said to stand for the blood shed for independence, hope, and the sun, as the source of life.

The coat of arms is the PAIGC badge, a black star and a scallop shell.

ARMS OF GUINEA-BISSAU

A star symbolizing African unity

The PAIGC motto – 'Unidade, Luta, Progresso' meaning 'Unity, Struggle, Progress'

As the PAIGC badge, the palm leaves represented Guinea-Bissau

The scallop shell originally recalled the Cape Verde islands

GUINEA

Ratio: 2:3 Adopted: *10 November 1958* Usage: *National and Civil*

Yellow represents
the sun and the
riches of the earth

Green represents
the country's
vegetation

The flag is
modelled on the
French Tricolore,
but in pan-
African colours

Red symbolizes the people's sacrifice

AFRICA

Senegal *Mali*
Guinea- **GUINEA**
Bissau
Sierra Leone *Ivory Coast*

IN 1958, GUINEA became the first territory in
former French West Africa to gain independence
without first becoming an autonomous republic.

The colours of the flag were adapted
from those of the *Rassemblement
Démocratique Africaine*, the dominant
movement at the time of
independence. Their colours were in
turn derived from those of Ghana,
which had first adopted them in
1957. Sekour Touré, the first
President of Guinea, was a close

associate of Kwame Nkrumah, the
former dictator of Ghana.

ARMS OF GUINEA

The coat of arms has been altered
since the fall of Sekour Touré. The
elephant's head was dropped and it
now portrays a dove above an olive
branch and crossed weapons.

ARMS OF GUINEA

The weapons recall
periods of war

The olive branch
symbolizes peace

The dove is a
symbol of peace

The national motto
'Travail, Justice,
Solidarité', meaning
'Work, Justice,
Solidarity'

TRAVAIL   SOLIDARITE
JUSTICE

SIERRA LEONE

Ratio: 2:3   Adopted: 27 April 1961   Usage: National and Civil

Green represents the agricultural and natural resources of the country

White stands for justice

Blue recalls the natural harbour at Freetown, the capital

AFRICA

SIERRA LEONE was founded as a home for freed slaves in 1787, but became a British colony in 1808. It achieved independence in 1961.

The arms and flag of Sierra Leone were devised by the College of Arms and granted in 1960.

ARMS OF SIERRA LEONE
The shield depicts a lion beneath a zigzag border, representing the Lion Mountains after which the territory was named, and three torches. At the base are wavy bars depicting the sea. The supporters are lions, similar to those on the colonial badge.

The three main colours from the shield – green, white and blue – were used to form the flag. They represent agricultural and natural resources in green, unity and justice in white, and blue for the harbour at Freetown.

ARMS OF SIERRA LEONE

The torches symbolize education and progress

National motto – 'Unity, Freedom, Justice'

The lions holding oil-palms are taken from the old colonial badge

The border represents the Lion Mountains

The wavy bars depict the sea

LIBERIA

Ratio: *10:19*   Adopted: *26 July 1847*   Usage: *National and Civil*

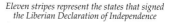

The star represents African freedom

The flag is modelled on the US Stars and Stripes

Eleven stripes represent the states that signed the Liberian Declaration of Independence

AFRICA

LIBERIA WAS FOUNDED in 1816 by the American Colonization Society as a home for freed slaves from the USA. It became independent in 1847.

The flag of Liberia is clearly based on that of the USA, with one white star in a blue canton standing for the freedom it was intended should shine forth in the so-called 'Dark Continent'. The canton itself represents Africa. The eleven stripes are said to stand, in this case, for the signatories of Liberia's Declaration of Independence.

All the counties of Liberia have local flags, but the extent of their use is unclear.

THE PRESIDENT'S FLAG
There is also a flag for the President, using a shield in the form of the national flag. Whether this is actually in use is in doubt, in view of the civil war in Liberia since 1990.

THE PRESIDENT'S FLAG

Four stars representing the Supreme Commander

Shield is derived from features of the national flag

IVORY COAST

Ratio: 2:3   Adopted: *3 December 1959*   Usage: *National and Civil*

Orange represents the savannah grasslands

Green recalls their coastal forests

The design is modelled on the French Tricolore

White represents the country's rivers

AFRICA

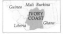

THE IVORY COAST was originally part of French West Africa. It became independent in its own right on 7 August 1960.

After independence, the Ivory Coast formed a loose alliance of West African states. The flags of these states were influenced both by the pan-African colours first used by Ghana, and also by the model of the French *Tricolore*, the flag of the former colonial power.

ALLIANCE OF WEST AFRICAN STATES
The colours chosen for the Ivory Coast's flag were also used by Niger, with which Ivory Coast had an alliance (the resemblance to the colours of Ireland is coincidental). They were intended to symbolize the following: orange represents the savannah grasslands, white the rivers and green the coastal forests.

Another interpretation is that they symbolize progress, hope and national unity. The flag was adopted in 1959, just prior to independence.

THE NATIONAL ARMS
The coat of arms, which has a green shield charged with an elephant's head, is based on the emblem of the *Rassemblement Démocratique Africaine*, the dominant political party at the time of independence. Originally the elephant's head was on a blue shield, but this was altered in 1964 to green, to match the national flag. The shield is supported by two palm trees. Behind is a rising sun. On a scroll at the base of the arms is the title of the state, *'Republique de Côte d'Ivoire'*.

BURKINA

Ratio: 2:3   Adopted: 4 August 1984   Usage: National and Civil

Red recalls the 1984 revolution

The star is the guiding light of the revolution

Red, yellow and green are pan-African colours

Green represents Burkina's abundant natural resources

BURKINA, originally known as Upper Volta, was once a French colony. It became self-governing in 1958 and fully independent in 1960.

The original flag of Upper Volta, adopted at independence, contained three horizontal stripes of black, white and red. These simple colours represented the three major tributaries of the Volta River, which flow south through the country.

A NEW NATIONAL FLAG
In August 1984 there was a coup and a new flag and emblem were adopted. The new flag is in the pan-African colours, reflecting both a break with the country's colonial past and its unity with other African ex-colonies. The red is also said to symbolize the revolution and the green the abundance of natural riches. The yellow star placed over

the red and green stripes is the guiding light of the revolution.

THE NATIONAL ARMS
The coat of arms shows a cog-wheel and a star to represent the revolution of 1984. Within the cog-wheel is a hoe representing agriculture, crossed with a Kalashnikov rifle symbolizing a willingness to defend the country and a book reflecting the importance of education. These are placed together to represent the alliance of workers, soldiers and intellectuals. Around the cog-wheel are sorghum plants. At the base is a scroll with the national motto – 'La Patrie Ou La Mort – Nous Vaincrons' ('Our country or death – We will conquer').

GHANA

Ratio: 2:3   Adopted: 6 March 1957   Usage: National

Red recalls the blood shed by freedom fighters

Ghana was the first country to use the pan-African colours of red, yellow, green and black

Yellow represents mineral wealth

Green is symbolic of the country's rich forests

The star of African freedom

AFRICA

PREVIOUSLY the Gold Coast, Ghana became independent from Britain in 1957. It took its new name from that of an historic African empire.

Kwame Nkrumah, Ghana's first leader after independence, was the first to introduce the politically symbolic pan-African colours – red, yellow, green and black – into African flags. They were ultimately derived from the colours of Ethiopia, dating back to the 19th century and have now become associated with the Rastafarian movement in the West Indies. The flag also became the inspiration for numerous other African flags during the period of decolonization.

Ghana followed the flag patterns established in the United Kingdom, and so has a both a red ensign for use on civil vessels and a white ensign for naval vessels. This use of several flags sets it apart from other West African states, which normally have only one all-purpose flag.

GHANAIAN RED ENSIGN

The national flag is placed in the canton

The field is in the style of the British Red Ensign

TOGO

Ratio: 2:3   Adopted: *27 April 1960*   Usage: *National and Civil*

The star of hope

Red symbolizes the blood shed during the struggle for independence

Green represents agricultural wealth

Yellow reflects Togo's mineral wealth

The five stripes represent the five regions of Togo

TOGO, once a German colony, was divided between France and Britain in 1914. The French part became independent, as Togo, in 1960.

During the period of autonomy 1956–1960 the flag was green with two yellow stars arranged diagonally with the French *Tricolore* in the canton.

On independence in 1960, the present flag was adopted. The five stripes stand for the regions of Togo, and are in green and yellow to signify its agricultural and mineral resources. The red canton is for the blood of those who struggled for independence, while the white star is for hope, as on Liberia's flag.

The national emblem contains two lions holding bows and arrows, and a sun with the country's initials. Above the sun is the national motto.

EMBLEM OF TOGO

The national motto – 'Union, Paix, Solidarité', meaning 'Unity, Peace, Solidarity'

'RT' stands for the title of the state 'République Togolaise'

Two lions are shown carrying bows and arrows to protect the homeland

BENIN

Ratio: 2:3   Adopted: *16 November 1959*   Usage: *National and Civil*

Red, yellow and green are pan-African colours

The colours symbolize African unity and nationalism

ORIGINALLY KNOWN as Dahomey, Benin became autonomous in 1958 and independent from France in 1960. Its name was changed in 1975.

The flag used today is the same as that adopted in 1959, although after the revolution of December 1975, a green flag with a red star in the canton was used. The original flag was restored in 1990, as was the original national emblem. The new name of the country was retained.

Benin has both a seal and a coat of arms. The seal depicts a *pirogue* or African canoe with a bow and arrow, and two clubs. The arms consists of a quartered shield depicting a local Somba fortress, the medal of the Order of the Star of Benin, a palm tree and a sailing ship. The motto is '*Fraternité, Justice, Travail* ' meaning 'Fraternity, Justice, Work'.

ARMS OF BENIN

The Horns of Plenty spilling out ears of corn are symbolic of riches from the land

The Order of Star of Benin

The national motto meaning 'Fraternity, Justice, Work'

A Somba fortress

NIGERIA

Ratio: *1:2*   Adopted: *1 October 1960*   Usage: *National*

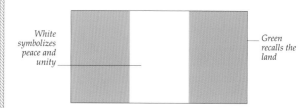

White symbolizes peace and unity

Green recalls the land

NIGERIA WAS FORMED in 1914 from several British colonies and protectorates. In 1954 it became a federation and in 1960 achieved independence.

The national flag is an adaptation of the winning entry in a competition held in 1959. The original had a red sun with streaming rays placed at the top of the white stripe. This was removed by the judges and the flag has not been altered since.

Like Ghana, Nigeria has special flags for civil and naval vessels and at one time the states also had flags.

The coat of arms was granted in 1960, but the motto has been altered since then to include the words 'Peace and Progress'. The shield represents the confluence of two rivers and the crest is a red eagle. It all stands on a green base strewn with the *Coctus spectabilis* flower.

ARMS OF NIGERIA

The red eagle symbolizing strength is the national badge

The Coctus spectabilis is the national flower

The confluence of the Niger and Benue rivers

The two white horses symbolize dignity

The national motto – 'Unity and Faith, Peace and Progress'

UNITY AND FAITH, PEACE AND PROGRESS

90

CAMEROON

Ratio: 2:3   Adopted: 20 May 1975   Usage: National and Civil

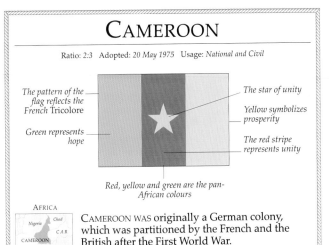

The pattern of the flag reflects the French Tricolore

Green represents hope

The star of unity

Yellow symbolizes prosperity

The red stripe represents unity

Red, yellow and green are the pan-African colours

AFRICA

CAMEROON WAS **originally a German colony, which was partitioned by the French and the British after the First World War.**

The French area became autonomous on 1 January 1959 and independent a year later. A national flag was adopted during the period of French control and was the first West African flag after that of Ghana to use the red, yellow and green colours. The actual design is based on the French *Tricolore*. The original design of 1959 did not have a star.

A NEW UNITED FLAG

In 1961, the southern part of British Cameroon joined the former French colony forming the current state of Cameroon. To mark this, two yellow stars were placed in the upper hoist. In 1975, the two stars were replaced by a single star in the centre of the flag to symbolize the new unity of the state.

THE NATIONAL ARMS

The coat of arms, like the flag, has been altered to reflect the changes in the constitution. The date on the original upper scroll reflected the date of independence of French Cameroon. This has now been removed, leaving just the name of the state on the scroll and there is now only one yellow star in the green on the shield. The main features of the current arms are a map of the country, a balance, and two crossed fasces or local axes. The shield is divided in the colours of the national flag; green, red and

91

EQUATORIAL GUINEA

Ratio: 2:3   Adopted: 12 October 1968   Usage: National and Civil

The blue triangle represents the sea

White stands for peace

Green reflects the country's agricultural lands

The national arms have always appeared on the flag

Red symbolizes the country's independence

AFRICA

EQUATORIAL GUINEA **includes the former Spanish colonies of Río Muni, the island of Fernando Po (Bioko) and other islands in the Gulf of Guinea.**

The flag was first shown on the day of independence, 12 October 1968, and has always contained the national emblem in the centre, although from 1972, during the regime of Francisco Nguema, a different national emblem appeared on the flag. The original coat of arms was restored after he was deposed in August 1979.

ARMS OF EQUATORIAL GUINEA
The arms consists of a silver shield charged with a silk-cotton tree, which was derived from the arms of Río Muni. Above the shield is an arc of six, six-pointed stars, which represent Río Muni and the offshore islands. Beneath the shield is a scroll with the national motto.

ARMS OF EQUATORIAL GUINEA

The six stars stand for the six parts of the state

A silk-cotton tree

The national motto – 'Unidad, Paz, Justicia' ('Unity, Peace, Justice')

A silver shield

SAO TOME & PRINCIPE

Ratio: 1:2 Adopted: 5 November 1975 Usage: National and Civil

The red triangle recalls the struggle for independence, as on the flags of Ghana and Togo

Green, red, yellow and black are pan-African colours

The two stars stand for the two islands

SÃO TOMÉ AND PRÍNCIPE are a pair of islands in the Gulf of Guinea that formerly belonged to Portugal. They became independent in 1975.

The flag is based on the party flag of the Movement for the Liberation of Sao Tome and Principe (MLSTP). It was retained even after the party lost its monopoly of power in 1990.

The combination of red, yellow and green with black stars, is clearly based on the flag of Ghana, with the stars standing for the two islands.

The shield within the national arms is in the form of a cocoa pod, on which is depicted a cocoa palm, the country's main export. Above this is a star representing freedom. The supporters are two pigeons standing on a scroll with the national motto – 'Unidade, Disciplina, Trabajo' ('Unity, Discipline, Work').

ARMS OF SAO TOME AND PRINCIPE

The crest, a blue star, stands for African freedom

The shield is in the form of a cocoa pod

The upper scroll bears the title of the state

The national motto – 'Unidade, Disciplina, Trabajo' ('Unity, Discipline, Work')

GABON

Ratio: 3:4   Adopted: *9 August 1960*   Usage: *National and Civil*

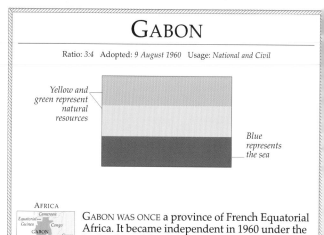

Yellow and green represent natural resources

Blue represents the sea

AFRICA

GABON WAS ONCE a province of French Equatorial Africa. It became independent in 1960 under the leadership of the Gabon Democratic Party.

The original flag was adopted in 1959 and was similar to the present one, but with stripes of unequal width and the French *Tricolore* in the canton. The *Tricolore* was dropped at independence. The flag's unusual proportions are laid down by law and the colours are said to stand for the sea, and for the country's natural resources, especially its timber.

The coat of arms is of European style and is in the colours of the flag. The shield is supported by two black panthers and an *okoumé* tree, symbolic of the timber trade. The coat of arms is unusual in having a Latin motto – '*Uniti Progrediamur*', beneath the branches of the tree.

ARMS OF GABON

A Latin motto – 'Unite Progrediamur' meaning 'We go forward in Unity'

A second motto means 'Union, Work, Justice'

The okoumé tree is symbolic of the timber trade

Two black panthers support the shield

The ship represents Gabon moving toward a brighter future

CONGO

Ratio: 2:3   Adopted: *20 November 1959*   Usage: *National and Civil*

The pan-African colours of red, yellow and green

The distinctive diagonal pattern sets it apart from other pan-African flags

AFRICA

CONGO WAS A French colony until independence as Congo-Brazzaville in 1960. After a coup in 1964, it became the People's Republic (1970–91).

The current flag was originally adopted for the autonomous republic, established on 18 August 1959. It is in the pan-African colours used by many other West African flags. It was retained without change when full independence was achieved in 1960.

THE PEOPLE'S REPUBLIC 1970–91
Following the Marxist revolution in 1964, no new national flag was officially adopted until the People's Republic was formed in 1970. This flag was red and contained the national emblem in the canton. The emblem depicted a wreath containing a crossed hoe and hammer, and a gold star. This represented the communist regime which had taken power.

AN OLD FLAG FOR A NEW ERA
At the National Conference for the restoration of democracy in 1991, which restored a multiparty democracy, it was decided to re-adopt the original flag, arms and national anthem. This decision was made official on 4 June 1991.

ARMS OF CONGO
The coat of arms was originally adopted in 1963 and was designed by the European heraldist Louis Mühlemann, who also designed the arms of Gabon. It follows a traditional European heraldic style.

ANGOLA

Ratio: 2:3 Adopted: 11 November 1975 Usage: National and Civil

The cog-wheel and machete are emblems of agriculture and of industry

The design is based on flag of the MPLA

The emblems are similar to the Soviet-style hammer and sickle

AFRICA

ORIGINALLY A PORTUGUESE COLONY, Angola was eventually liberated by the People's Liberation Movement of Angola in 1975.

The flag of the People's Liberation Movement of Angola (MPLA) is like the present national flag but with a yellow star. The half cog-wheel and machete on the national flag were added, to create an emblem reminiscent of the hammer and sickle on the Soviet flag.

The national arms also features the cog-wheel, star and machete, but includes a hoe. These symbols are placed on a background which, like the emblem on the flag, is similar to the devices used in Soviet designs. The cog-wheel is balanced by a wreath of cotton, coffee and maize, and an open book. On the scroll is 'Republic of Angola', the state name.

ARMS OF ANGOLA

These are emblems of agriculture and of industry

The book is symbolic of the importance of education

The Soviet-style emblem is still in use

The state name, in Portuguese – República de Angola – is placed on the scroll

REPÚBLICA DE ANGOLA

ZAMBIA

Ratio: 2:3   Adopted: 24 October 1964   Usage: National and Civil

The green field represents Zambia's agriculture

The eagle is taken from the national arms

Yellow represents the country's copper

Red recalls the struggle for independence   *Black stands for the people*

AFRICA

ZAMBIA WAS FORMERLY the British colony of Northern Rhodesia. It was granted full independence in 1964.

Although the United National Independence Party is no longer dominant in Zambia, the party's colours remain in the bottom left of the flag, designed by graphic artists just prior to independence. The eagle is taken from the national arms, which are based on those of the former Northern Rhodesia.

In the arms, the eagle, which once appeared in the upper part of the shield, forms the crest, above a crossed pickaxe and hoe. White and black bars on the shield represent the famous Victoria Falls. The supporters are an African man and woman and the motto on the base reads 'One Zambia, One Nation'.

ARMS OF ZAMBIA

The eagle of liberty

The pickaxe and hoe are emblems of agriculture and industry

The shield stands on an allegorical landscape

The shield represents the white waters of the Zambezi River flowing over black rock at the Victoria Falls

ONE ZAMBIA   ONE NATION

TANZANIA

Ratio: 2:3   Adopted: *30 June 1964*   Usage: *National and Civil*

*Green and black,
taken from the old
Tanganyikan flag,
represent the land
and the people*

*Blue, taken
from the flag
of Zanzibar,
represents
the sea*

*Yellow symbolizes
mineral wealth*

THE BRITISH TRUSTEESHIP TERRITORY of Tanganyika
became independent in 1961. In 1964, it merged
with the Republic of Zanzibar, to form Tanzania.

The original flag of independent
Tanganyika was derived from that of
the Tanganyika African National
Union, the dominant party at the
time. This was horizontal stripes of
green-black-green. For the national
flag, yellow fimbriations were placed
between the green and the black.

Derived from the Afro-Shirazi
Party, the flag of Zanzibar is green,
black and blue stripes, with a vertical

white stripe along the hoist.

A NEW UNITED FLAG

When the two countries united to
form Tanzania, a new national flag
was created which combined the
colours of Tanganyika and Zanzibar.
The country's coat of arms was also
altered to include the new national
flag in the shield, again to reflect the
new union of the two countries.

FLAG OF ZANZIBAR

*Blue was incorporated in
the new national flag
of Tanzania*

*A white fimbriation
runs along the hoist*

*These are the colours
of the Afro-Shirazi
Party, who overthrew
the ruling Sultan
in 1964*

MALAWI

Ratio: 2:3   Adopted: 6 July 1964   Usage: National and Civil

Black is symbolic of Malawi's African heritage

The rising sun symbolizes a new dawn

Red represents the blood shed for freedom

Green represents the land

These are the colours of the Malawi Congress Party

AFRICA

As NYASALAND, Malawi formed part of British Rhodesia and Nyasaland from 1953–63. It became fully independent in 1964.

The colours of the flag are the same as those of Malawi Congress Party (MCP) which led the country to independence in 1964. The MCP flag was derived from the flag popularized by Marcus Garvey (*see page 7*) at the time of the First World War, as the flag of Africa or 'Ethiopia', symbolizing an African renaissance. For Malawi's national flag the rising sun or *kwacha* was added in red. The *kwacha* also appeared on the colonial coat of arms adopted in 1914. It was retained on the current arms granted with the flag in 1964.

THE PRESIDENT'S FLAG

The flag of the President has a bright red field. It uses the lion passant found in the centre of the coat of arms, with the name 'Malawi'.

THE PRESIDENT'S FLAG

The name of the state

The lion passant is taken from the coat of arms

ZIMBABWE

Ratio: *1:2* Adopted: *18 April 1980* Usage: *National and Civil*

The national bird of Zimbabwe

Green, yellow, red and black are the colours of ZANU and pan-Africanism

Black represents the new leaders, and white, their desire for peace

AFRICA

ZIMBABWE, the name of an ancient African city, is now applied to the whole country, which was formerly known as Rhodesia.

The Zimbabwe African National Union (ZANU) led the struggle for self-determination in the 1970s, and its flag was used as the basis for the new national flag. The ZANU flag is composed of concentric panels of green, yellow, red, with a central black panel; the colours of pan-Africanism. The national flag has these colours simply arranged in stripes. Towards the hoist is a white triangle with a black edge, symbolizing new leaders and their desire for peace. Within this is the Zimbabwe bird on a red star.

THE ZIMBABWE BIRD
The bird is representative of birds found in the ruins of the ancient city of Zimbabwe and has been a local symbol since 1924. The star stands for an international outlook.

EMBLEM OF ZIMBABWE

The star represents the country's international outlook

The Zimbabwe bird

A representation of the ancient city of Zimbabwe

MOZAMBIQUE

Ratio: 2:3   Adopted: *1 May 1983*   Usage: *National and Civil*

Green symbolizes the riches of the land

Red recalls the struggle for independence

Black recalls the African continent

The white fimbriations represent peace

Yellow symbolizes the country's minerals

AFRICA

MOZAMBIQUE WAS A Portuguese colony before becoming independent under the single-party rule of FRELIMO in 1975.

The original flag of the *Frente da Libertação da Moçambique* (FRELIMO), the leading political party in Mozambique, also had green, black and yellow horizontal stripes separated by white fimbriations. In the hoist was a red triangle. The black, green and yellow were derived from the flag of the African National Congress, used in South Africa. On independence the colours were re-arranged to form the national flag, in rays emanating from the upper hoist. Over this was a white cog-wheel containing the hoe, rifle, book and star which appear on the present flag. The flag was altered in 1983; the colours were arranged in horizontal stripes, and the star of Marxism was made larger. It is likely that a new, non-partisan flag will be introduced.

EMBLEM OF MOZAMBIQUE

The hoe represents the country's agriculture

The star symbolizes Marxism and internationalism

The rifle stands for defence and vigilance

The open book symbolizes the importance of education

NAMIBIA

Ratio: 2:3   Adopted: *21 March 1990*   Usage: *National and Civil*

The sun is the emblem of life and energy

Red, white and blue were the colours of the Democratic Turnhalle Alliance

Blue, red and green were the colours of SWAPO

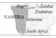

NAMIBIA, once German South West Africa, passed into South African control after the First World War, until gaining independence in 1990.

The national flag combines the colours of the South West African People's Organization (SWAPO), which liberated Namibia in 1990, and those of the Democratic Turnhalle Alliance, another Namibian political party. The sun, which is similar to that on the flag of Taiwan, is said to stand for life and energy.

ARMS OF NAMIBIA
The coat of arms, adopted with the flag, appears on the President's Flag. The shield is of the same pattern as the national flag, and is supported by a pair of oryx. On a sand-dune beneath is a *welwitschia* plant, found in the Namib Desert. The crest is a fish eagle on a chieftain's head-ring.

ARMS OF NAMIBIA

The fish eagle stands on a chieftain's head-ring

The shield is based on the national flag

Two oryx support the shield

The welwitschia plant is found in the Namib Desert

The national motto – 'Unity, Liberty, Justice'

BOTSWANA

Ratio: 2:3   Adopted: *30 September 1966*   Usage: *National and Civil*

Black and white symbolize the harmony of the people

Blue represents both water and life

BOTSWANA, originally known as British Bechuanaland, is now known by its Setswana name. Independence was achieved in 1966.

Unusually for Africa, the national flag of Botswana is not derived from that of the dominant political party. Neither does it use the pan-African colours.

PULA – LIFE-GIVING RAIN

Instead, it is based on the idea of life-giving rain, an essential element in the drought-prone country. This is also reflected in the Setswana word *pula,* which forms the national motto. This means not only 'water' and 'rain' but also the life that is derived from it.

The two horizontal blue stripes represent rain and water. The importance of water is also a feature on the flag of Lesotho. The black

stripe fimbriated with white in the centre of the flag represents the idea of the African and European populations of Botswana living together in harmony.

ARMS OF BOTSWANA

The coat of arms which appears on the President's Flag was adopted in 1966. The African shield depicts three cog-wheels and a bull's head separated by three wavy bars of water. The supporters are two zebras, holding an elephant tusk and a sorghum plant, the country's staple crop. Some also interpret the zebras, with their black and white stripes, as being symbolic of racial integration.

LESOTHO

Ratio: 2:3   Adopted: *20 January 1987*   Usage: *National and Civil*

A simplified version of the arms showing a shield, a spear and a local club

White represents peace

Green represents plenty

Blue is symbolic of the importance of water and rain

AFRICA

LESOTHO WAS FORMERLY known as British Basutoland but is now known by its Sesotho name. It became independent in 1966.

The flag hoisted on the day of independence was based on the colours of the then dominant Basuto National Party and depicted a typical African straw hat.

THE NEW NATIONAL FLAG
Following a *coup d'etat* in 1986, the original flag was discarded and the present flag adopted on 20 January 1987. Unlike its predecessor, it does not contain any political colours, but instead is intended to represent the words of the national motto: '*Khotso-Pula-Nala*', meaning 'Peace, Rain, Plenty', by the colours white, blue and green. Water is also symbolized on the national flag of Botswana. In the canton is a simplified version of part of the coat of arms which was adopted on independence in 1966.

ROYAL ARMS OF LESOTHO
On the national flag only the outline of the shield is shown, with its tufted spine, and two weapons, but on the Royal Standard the whole arms appear in colour.

The shield, of African design, contains a crocodile, which is a symbol of King Moshoeshoe I, who founded the state in 1824. It stands on a representation of Mount Thaba Bosiu, the Mountain of Night, and is supported by two Basuto ponies. Behind the shield is a spear and a *knobkerrie*, a local club.

SWAZILAND

Ratio: 2:3   Adopted: *30 October 1967*   Usage: *National and Civil*

Injobo *tassles, made from widowbird and loury feathers*

Assegais *are Swazi spears*

The pattern of the shield is taken from the Emasotsha Regiment

AFRICA

SWAZILAND was a British Protectorate until 1968. It is now ruled by the Swazi royal family who founded the kingdom in the 19th century.

The flag is based on one given by the late King Sobhuza II to the Swazi Pioneer Corps in 1941. On it are an Emasotsha shield, laid horizontally. The shield is reinforced by a staff from which hang *injobo* tassles; bunches of feathers of the widowbird and the loury. They also decorate the shield. Above the staff are two *assegais* – local spears. The shield and *assegais* appear on the national arms, which is supported by a lion and an elephant, symbolic of the King and of the Queen Mother. The crest is an otter-skin head-dress decorated with widowbird feathers, and the motto is '*Siyinqaba*' meaning 'We are the fortress'.

ARMS OF SWAZILAND

A lion, symbolic of the King

The national motto – 'We are the fortress'

A head-dress and widowbird feathers

An elephant, symbolic of the Queen Mother

SOUTH AFRICA

Ratio: 2:3 Adopted: 27 April 1994 Usage: National and Civil

The overall design conveys convergence and unification

Yellow, black and green are taken from the ANC flag

Red, white and blue are taken from the colours of the Boer republics

AFRICA

THE UNION OF SOUTH AFRICA was formed in 1910 and the republic in 1961. In 1994 a democratic, multi-racial constitution was adopted.

South Africa had no distinctive flag until 1928 when a national flag was adopted based on the orange, white and blue tricolour used by the first Dutch settlers, with three smaller flags in the centre for Britain, the Transvaal and the Orange Free State.

When a multi-racial democracy came into prospect, attempts were made to find a new flag and the present design, created by the Chief Herald of South Africa, was adopted.

A NEW FLAG FOR A NEW ERA
The new South African flag combines the colours of the Boer republics, with those of the African National Congress (ANC), whose flag was adopted in 1917. The Y-shape represents the convergence of old traditions with new and the progress of the united state into the future.

AFRICAN NATIONAL CONGRESS FLAG

Black represents the people

Green represents the land

Yellow symbolizes riches

SEYCHELLES

Ratio: 1:2   Adopted: 8 January 1996   Usage: National and Civil

The flag now includes blue and yellow, the colours of the Democratic Party

Red, white and green are the colours of the SPUP

AFRICA

THE SEYCHELLES became independent from France in 1976. In 1977, a *coup d'état* brought the Seychelles Peoples United Party to power.

The Seychelles has had three flags since independence. After the coup of 1977 a new national flag based on the party flag of the ruling SPUP was adopted. This used their colours of red, white and green.

Following the adoption of the Constitution of 1993, the existence of other parties was permitted and the latest flag allows for the colours of the Democratic Party to be included in a striking new design.

The coat of arms was adopted in 1976 and it has been only slightly altered since then. It is based on the old colonial badge and depicts the most famous inhabitant of the islands, the giant tortoise.

ARMS OF THE SEYCHELLES

Two sailfish support the arms

The giant tortoise and palm have been in use in the arms since the 19th century

The crest is a paille-en-queue, *a native bird of the Seychelles*

A Latin motto – 'Finis Coronat Opus', meaning 'The end crowns the work', was chosen in the 19th century

COMOROS

Ratio: 3:5   Adopted: 1997   Usage: Government and Civil

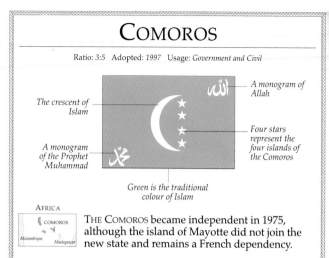

A monogram of Allah

The crescent of Islam

A monogram of the Prophet Muhammad

Four stars represent the four islands of the Comoros

Green is the traditional colour of Islam

AFRICA

THE COMOROS became independent in 1975, although the island of Mayotte did not join the new state and remains a French dependency.

The present flag is based on one adopted at independence, which included stars for the four main islands (including Mayotte) and a crescent to symbolize Islam. The original flag was red with a green stripe across the bottom. This was dropped in 1978 in favour of a green flag with the crescent and stars in white. At first the crescent was 'aimed' at the lower fly, but for a brief period during 1997 it was depicted on its back.

The Constitution of 1997 established the present form which also includes the monograms of Allah and of Muhammad in the corners. The crescent is now upright facing the fly, as is common in Muslim flags, where the object is to depict a growing rather than a diminishing crescent.

THE NATIONAL FLAG 1972–1997

Before 1997 the crescent and stars were placed at an angle

108

MADAGASCAR

Ratio: 2:3   Adopted: *14 October 1958*   Usage: *National and Civil*

Red and white were the colours of the Kingdom of Madagascar

Green represents the Hova, the former peasant class

MADAGASCAR was annexed by France in 1895 and the monarchy abolished two years later. It achieved independence in 1960.

The flag was introduced when self-government was achieved in 1958 and was retained on independence. The red and white are said to symbolize the earlier Merina Kingdom, whose flags were all red and white, with the addition of green for the Hova, the former peasant class. The coat of arms has changed several times since independence. That of the present republic, introduced in March 1993, shows a map of the island with a spray of leaves. Beneath these is a paddy field surmounted by the head of a zebu. The motto reads 'Fatherland, Liberty, Justice'. Above the design is the country name.

ARMS OF MADAGASCAR

The state title is in Malagasy, the local language

The national motto – 'Fatherland, Liberty, Justice'

The leaves of the traveller's tree

An outline of Madagascar

A stylized paddy field and a zebu, a local ox

MAURITIUS

Ratio: 2:3   Adopted: *9 January 1968*   Usage: *National*

Red reflects
independence

Blue is the
colour of the
Indian Ocean

Yellow symbolizes
a bright future

Green recalls the lush
vegetation of the island

AFRICA

MAURITIUS WAS TAKEN over by Britain from France
in 1810. The colony achieved independence in
1968 and became a republic in 1992.

The flag was designed by the College
of Arms in Britain prior to
independence, and is a simple
statement of the colours found in
the coat of arms.

ARMS OF MAURITIUS

The coat of arms was granted on
25 August 1906, and depicts various

attributes of the island. In the lower
right quarter is a key and on the left-
hand side is a white star, which are
referred to in the Latin motto, '*Stella
Clavisque Maris Indici*' ('The star and
the key of the Indian Ocean'). The
supporters are a dodo and a deer
each holding a sugar cane, the
island's staple crop.

ARMS OF MAURITIUS

A dodo, extinct since
the 18th century

A ship symbolizing
colonization

The star and key
are referred to
in the motto

Palm trees represent
the country's tropical
vegetation

A deer

The national motto –
'The star and the key of
the Indian Ocean'

ICELAND

Ratio: *18:25* Adopted: *19 June 1915* Usage: *National and Civil*

White recalls the ice and snow which covers Iceland

Deep blue represents the Atlantic Ocean

Red represents the fire produced by the island's volcanoes

EUROPE

RULED BY THE DANES from the 14th century, Iceland became a realm within the kingdom of Denmark in 1918, and a republic in 1944.

Iceland's first national flag was a white cross on a deep blue background. It was first paraded in 1897. The modern flag dates from 1915, when a red cross was inserted into the white cross of the original flag. It was adopted in 1918 and became the national flag when Iceland gained independence from Denmark in 1944.

FIRE, ICE AND WATER
For the Icelandic people the flag's colouring represents a vision of their country's landscape. The colours stand for three of the elements that make up the island: fire, ice and water.

The President's flag is a swallow-tailed flag with the national arms in the centre. It was adopted in 1944.

THE PRESIDENT'S FLAG

According to legend the figures on the shield are guardian spirits who defend the island from attack

Fantastical figures of a bull, eagle, dragon and giant

A swallow-tailed flag

NORWAY

Ratio: *8:11*   Adopted: *17 July 1821*   Usage: *National and Civil*

The red, white and blue colours were influenced by the French Tricolore – a symbol of liberty – and by the flags of the UK and USA

Off-centred white cross on a red field is taken from the Danish flag

The blue cross of Sweden

EUROPE

RULED BY DENMARK from 1397, Norway passed to Sweden in 1814. It gained independence in 1905, when its union with Sweden was dissolved.

Until 1814, the Norwegian flag bore the Danish red and white cross. The current flag was born in 1821, during the period when Norway was united with Sweden. The flag combines these two influences; its red and white colouring is taken from the Danish flag, and a blue cross was added overall. These three colours were chosen in honour of the French

Tricolore, a symbol of revolution and liberty. They were also the colours of the flags of the United States of America and the United Kingdom, two other countries that were not ruled by an absolute monarch.

The Royal Standard consists of a banner of the Royal Arms, dating back to the Middle Ages. It depicts a lion rampant on a red field.

THE ROYAL STANDARD

The standard dates back to the Middle Ages

A tall, slender lion bearing the axe of St Olav

DENMARK

Ratio: 28:37 Adopted: 1625 Usage: *National and Civil*

The off-centred cross is the basis for other Scandinavian countries' flags

According to legend, a red flag with a white cross 'appeared as a sign from heaven'

DENMARK IS EUROPE'S oldest kingdom, dating back to the 10th century. The present queen rules under a constitution granted in 1953.

Besides being the oldest monarchy in Europe, Denmark also has the oldest flag, known as the *Dannebrog*, or Danish cloth. Legend says that a blood-red flag with a white cross appeared as a sign from heaven to King Valdemar II during the conquest of Estonia in 1219. In reality, the flag may have been a gift from the Pope during the Crusades.

THE SCANDINAVIAN CROSS
The flag was originally square, but its design was elongated and the arm of the cross in the fly was extended. It has become a model for other flags.

Overseas Territories

FAEROE ISLANDS

The Faeroe Islands are a self-governing territory of Denmark. The flag has the Norwegian colours in a new arrangement. This recalls that they were once part of Norway.

GREENLAND

Greenland's flag was designed by a local artist and adopted in 1985. In the Danish colours, white represents the ice which covers most of the island and red is for the Sun.

SWEDEN

Ratio: 5:8   Adopted: 22 June 1906   Usage: National and Civil

The yellow and blue colours are taken from the national arms

The distinctive Scandinavian cross is taken from the flag of Denmark

EUROPE

UNTIL 1523, when King Gustav Vasa laid the foundation of Sweden as a separate state, the country was under the influence of Denmark.

The present flag was adopted in 1906, but it was first used in a similar form almost four centuries before. The design is based on the Scandinavian cross. The flag's blue and yellow colours are thought to come from the national coat of arms – three gold crowns in a blue field – which originated in the 14th century. A national flag day is celebrated each year on 6 June. On this day in 1523 King Gustav Vasa was elected and, on the same date in 1809, Sweden adopted a new constitution.

SWEDISH ROYAL STANDARD

The coat of arms is placed in the centre of the Royal Standard, which is used on special occasions by Parliament and dates from the 1440s.

THE ROYAL STANDARD

The shield is supported by two golden lions

The triple crown symbolizes the 'Three Wise Men', a Swedish emblem since 1336

FINLAND

Ratio: *11:18*   Adopted: *29 May 1918*   Usage: *National and Civil*

Blue represents Finland's blue skies and its thousands of lakes

The overall design is based on the Scandinavian cross

White recalls the snows of winter

FINLAND WAS PART OF Sweden from the 12th century. From 1809 until independence in 1917, it was part of the Russian Empire.

Like Sweden's, Finland's national flag is based on the Scandinavian cross. It was adopted after independence from Russia, when many patriotic Finns wanted a special flag for their country, but its design dates back to the 19th century. The blue colouring is said to represent the country's thousands of lakes and the sky, with white for the snow that covers the land in winter. This colour combination has also been used over the centuries in various Finnish provincial, military and town flags.

THE ÅLAND ISLANDS
The Åland Islands are an autonomous group of Finnish islands with their own flag since 1954. The design incorporates a Scandinavian cross.

THE FLAG OF THE ÅLAND ISLANDS

Red and yellow are taken from the arms of Finland

Blue and yellow represent Sweden; the islands have a large Swedish population

ESTONIA

Ratio: 7:11 Adopted: 8 May 1990 Usage: *National and Civil*

Blue represents loyalty and Estonia's sky, sea and lakes

White represents virtue, the snow and Estonia's struggle for freedom

Black is symbolic of past oppression and the soil

EUROPE

AFTER THE SECOND WORLD WAR, Estonia became a republic within the Soviet Union. It gained independence from the Soviet Union in 1991.

The tricolour was first adopted by students in 1881 during uprisings against occupying Russian Tsarist forces. It was re-adopted as the national flag in 1990 just prior to independence. The colours represent Estonian history, folk costumes, and landscape. Blue is the colour of loyalty and also represents the sky, sea and lakes. Black symbolizes the past suffering of the people, the soil and the traditional black peasant's jacket. White represents virtue and the struggle for freedom. It is also the colour of birch bark and snow.

The great coat of arms was originally the emblem of a 13th-century Danish king.

GREAT ARMS OF ESTONIA

The shield is surrounded by golden branches of oak

Three blue leopards are ranged on a gold shield

LATVIA

Ratio: 1:2   Adopted: *27 February 1990*   Usage: *National and Civil*

White may
stand for the
sheet used to
wrap the
wounded
Latvian
leader

Red
recalls the
blood shed
by the
wounded
leader

Red also represents Latvians'
willingness to defend their liberty

EUROPE

OVER THE CENTURIES, Latvia has been invaded by
Swedes, Poles and Russians. It became
independent from the Soviet Union in 1991.

Though officially adopted in 1922,
the Latvian flag was in use as early
as the 13th century, but its use was
suppressed during Soviet rule.

The red colour is sometimes
described as symbolizing the
readiness of the Latvians to give the
blood from their hearts for freedom.
An alternative interpretation,

according to one legend, is that a
Latvian leader was wounded in
battle, and the edges of the white
sheet in which he was wrapped were
stained by his blood.

The coat of arms depicts a tripartite
shield recalling the three reunited
duchies of Latvia. The shield is held
by a red lion and a silver griffin.

ARMS OF LATVIA

Three stars for the
reunited duchies

Rising sun
represents the
Duchy of Latgale

The red lion
represents the
Duchy of Kurzeme

The silver griffin
recalls the Duchy of
Vidzeme

LITHUANIA

Ratio: *1:2* Adopted: *20 March 1989* Usage: *National and Civil*

Yellow represents wheat and freedom from want

Green symbolizes the forests and renewed hope

Red symbolizes patriotism and courage

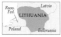

AFTER DECLARING independence from Russia in 1918, Lithuania was again occupied by the Soviet Union in 1940. It declared independence in 1991.

The national flag dates from the independent republic of 1918–1940. It was suppressed under the Soviet regime, but was re-adopted in 1990. Yellow is said to stand for ripening wheat, green for the forests and red for love of the country, or alternatively for the blood shed in defence of the nation. Red also refers to the colour of the medieval banners of the kingdom of Lithuania. Together, the colours stand for hope, courage and freedom from want.

ARMS OF LITHUANIA

The coat of arms' red shield dates from the 14th century. It was re-adopted in 1991.

ARMS OF LITHUANIA

A white knight on his charger

The double-barred cross commemorates the conversion of Grand Duke Jaggelon of Lithuania to Catholicism in 1386, at the time of his marriage to Queen Hedwig of Poland

POLAND

Ratio: 5:8   Adopted: 1 August 1919   Usage: National

The bicolour design was adopted after the First World War

White represents a desire for peace

In the past red was said to represent socialism

Red and white were taken from the 13th century arms

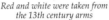

EUROPE

POLAND IS strategically placed in Europe and its borders have constantly shifted. They were last altered after the Second World War in 1945.

The red and white colours of the flag have been used since the 13th century, although they did not became the official national colours until 1831. They were taken from the colours of the national arms, first recorded in 1228.

THE NATIONAL ARMS

The coat of arms traditionally shows a white eagle on a red field. This emblem has remained more or less unchanged throughout Poland's turbulent history. The coat of arms was used by the Kingdom of Poland until its fall in 1795, and was re-adopted by the newly-declared republic around 1918/19, when a zigzag border and crown were added. The border and the crown were both dropped under the communist administration, but the crown was restored in 1993.

THE PEOPLE'S REPUBLIC OF POLAND

Under communist rule from 1945–1989, white was commonly said to represent the people's desire for peace, and during this period, red stood for socialism. The flag was re-confirmed as the national flag by the new government in 1992.

The plain bicoloured flag is used for general purposes on land. When at sea the flag is charged with the state arms in the centre. Poland also has a swallow-tailed ensign, which is also charged with the state arms.

GERMANY

Ratio: *3:5*   Adopted: *23 May 1949*   Usage: *National and Civil*

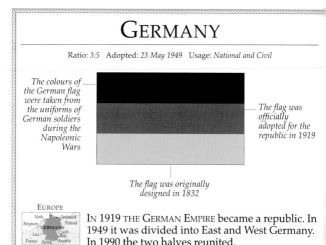

The colours of the German flag were taken from the uniforms of German soldiers during the Napoleonic Wars

The flag was officially adopted for the republic in 1919

The flag was originally designed in 1832

EUROPE

IN 1919 THE GERMAN EMPIRE became a republic. In 1949 it was divided into East and West Germany. In 1990 the two halves reunited.

Until the 19th century, Germany was a collection of feudal states. In 1848 an attempt was made to unite them, and although no union was established, a flag was produced. This was a black, red and gold horizontal tricolour. The colours were taken from the uniforms of the German soldiers in the Napoleonic Wars in the late 18th century.

THE GERMAN EMPIRE

Most of the states finally united into the German Empire in 1871, but instead of retaining the black, red and gold flag, the rival Bismarck tricolour of black, white and red was adopted. This was a combination of the red of the Hanseatic League and the black and white of Prussia, of which Bismarck was Chancellor.

THE *WEIMAR* REPUBLIC

After Germany's defeat in the First World War a republic was declared in 1919 and the black, red and gold flag returned. Its revival was short-lived and in 1933, when the Nazi government came to power they restored the imperial colours and made their party flag, the *Hakenkreuz*, the national flag.

After the Second World War, both German states reverted to using the black, red and gold tricolour, but East Germany added its coat of arms. Since reunification, the plain tricolour has been used.

Germany – Länder flags

ON GERMAN REGIONAL FLAGS the arms only appear on the official versions (except Lower Saxony, Saarland and Rhineland Palatinate).

BADEN-WÜRTTEMBURG

The flag was adopted in 1953. Its colours derive from the arms of Duke Frederick V of Swabia, the coat of arms dates back to 1265. It was adopted as the state arms in 1954.

BERLIN

The flag was first adopted for West Berlin in 1950 and extended to the whole city in 1991. The bear, a pun on the name Berlin, dates from 1338 and the colours from 1861.

BREMEN

The flag of Bremen predates its coat of arms, which was adopted in 1891. Prior to this, Bremen was a member of the Hanseatic League, where the flag originated.

HESSEN

The flag of Hessen was adopted 1948. The coat of arms was that of Ludwig III of Thuringia in 1182. The red and white colours of the flag are taken from the lion in the arms.

BAVARIA

Bavaria's flag was adopted in 1950, but blue and white have been Bavarian colours since 1330 and the lozenge shapes first appeared on banners in the 15th century.

BRANDENBURG

The colours of the flag are from the shield, dating from 1170, although red and white were also the colours of the medieval Hanseatic League. The flag was adopted in 1990.

HAMBURG

Used since 1325, red and white are the Hanseatic colours. The castle is for Hamburg; the three towers for the Trinity; the cross for Christ; the stars for the Father and Holy Spirit.

LOWER SAXONY

This flag uses the national flag with Lower Saxony's local arms in the centre. It was adopted in 1946, but the arms dates from 1361, when it appeared on the seal of the ruler.

MECKLENBURG-VORPOMMERN

This flag, adopted in 1991, combines blue and white of Pomerania with blue, yellow and red of Mecklenburg. The bull and the gryphon are also local emblems. Red and white recall the Hanseatic League.

 NORTH-RHINE-WESTPHALIA

The coat of arms depicts the River Rhine of the Rhineland, the horse of Westphalia and the rose of Lippe; the three territories which united to form the the state. The colours of the flag are from the arms.

 RHINELAND-PALATINATE

The flag was adopted in 1948 when the arms were placed on the national flag. The coat of arms depicts the lion of the Palatinate dating from 1229, the cross of Trier from 1273 and the wheel of Mainz from 1335.

 SAARLAND

Adopted in 1957, the flag of Saarland recalls the different parts of the state. Depicted on the shield is the lion of Saarbrücken, the cross of Trier, the eagles of Lorraine and the lion of Pfalz-Zweibrücken.

 SAXONY

The flag was adopted in 1991, but the coat of arms is the traditional arms of the rulers of Saxony; black and yellow bands and the green crown of rue. The white and green flag dates from the 19th century.

 SAXONY-ANHALT

This flag was the same as Baden-Württemberg until 1991, when the colours were reversed. The eagle recalls Prussia, the bicoloured bands and rue crown, Saxony, and the bear and wall are the arms of Anhalt.

 SCHLESWIG-HOLSTEIN

The shield depicts two lions from arms of Schleswig and a nettle-leaf from those of Holstein. The colours of the flag, adopted in 1957, are taken from the arms.

 THURINGIA

Another flag whose colours are based on the state arms. It was adopted in 1991. The red and white lion was the arms of the Counts of Thuringia in the 12th century.

THE NETHERLANDS

Ratio: 2:3   Adopted: *19 February 1937*   Usage: *National and Civil*

Blue and white, along with the original orange, were the livery colours of William of Orange

In the mid-17th century, red, rather than orange, was made the official colour

EUROPE

INDEPENDENT FROM SPAIN in the 16th century, the Netherlands was a republic until the Napoleonic Wars and became a kingdom in 1814.

The first *Stadtholder*, or ruler, of the Dutch Republic was William of Orange, who joined with Dutch nationalists and led the struggle for independence from Spain.

THE *PRINSVLAG*
Partly out of respect for him, the first flag adopted by the Dutch, was a horizontal tricolour of orange, white and blue *(see page 6)*. It became known as the *Prinsvlag* and was based on the livery of William of Orange. The orange dye was particularly unstable and tended to turn red after a while, so in the mid-17th century, red was made the official colour. The flag has flown since then, but was only confirmed

by Royal Decree in 1937. As the first revolutionary flag, it has had a seminal influence throughout the world, particularly on the pan-Slavic colours of Russia.

Until about 1800, in the case of both the orange- and red-striped versions, the number of stripes and their order frequently varied.

ARMS OF THE NETHERLANDS
The Dutch coat of arms depicts a golden lion on a blue shield, holding a sword and a sheaf of arrows. It is a combination of the coat of arms of the Dutch Republic and that of the House of Orange. The seven arrows represent the seven original provinces in the Netherlands.

The Netherlands – Provincial flags

EXCEPTING FLEVOLAND, all the Dutch provincial flags originate in traditional flags or arms going back in some cases to the 15th century.

 DRENTHE

White and red are the colours of the Archbishops of Utrecht, former rulers of Drenthe. The black castle and stars recall the uprising of Coevorden against the archbishop.

 FLEVOLAND

Blue is for the Lake Ijssel from which the province was reclaimed. Green is for vegetation and yellow for the cornfields. The lily recalls Lely the engineer of the reclamation project.

 FRIESLAND

The flag is based on that of the 15th century kings of Friesland. The colours are those of the Dutch flag. The stripes and flowers represent the seven districts of Friesland.

 GELDERLAND

In 1371, the dukedoms of Gelre and Gulik were united and combined their arms. The new arms was blue, yellow and black, the colours which appear in the flag, hoisted in 1953.

 GRONINGEN

The flag, adopted in 1950, combines green and white from the town of Groningen, surrounded by red, white and blue of Ommeland, reflecting the town's position.

 LIMBURG

The red lion is from the arms of Limburg. White and yellow are from local coats of arms, while the narrow blue stripe is for the River Maas which crosses the province.

 NORTH BRABANT

The design, adopted in 1959, originated in Antwerp where red and white checked coats of arms were popular. It was associated with the area from the 17th century.

 NORTH HOLLAND

Adopted in 1958, this flag unites the colours of Holland; yellow and red, with blue and yellow of West Friesland. Yellow, the common colour, is placed at the top.

OVERIJSSEL

The yellow and red stripes recall the ancient association of the province with Holland. The wavy blue stripe running across the centre is for the Ijssel River, after which the province is named.

SOUTH HOLLAND

The flag is a banner of the arms of Holland and was adopted in this form in 1986, replacing the previous simple triband of yellow-red-yellow, which was also based on the colours of the arms .

UTRECHT

The Archbishop of Utrecht used a red flag with a white cross from 1528. The Archbishop's flag remains in the canton of the modern flag, adopted in 1952. The field is in the traditional colours of the province.

ZEELAND

The flag of Zeeland, adopted in 1949, shows its full coat of arms. The wavy blue and white stripes are for the sea and the constant struggle to control it. From the water, the Dutch lion rises in triumph.

ARUBA

The flag of Aruba was adopted in 1976 when it was still administered as part of the Netherlands Antilles. The flag was retained when Aruba became autonomous in 1986.

NETHERLANDS ANTILLES

Originally adopted in 1959, the flag incorporated the Dutch colours with six stars on the blue stripe, for the island groups. These were reduced to five in 1986 when Aruba left the Netherlands Antilles.

BELGIUM

Ratio: *13:15* Adopted: *23 January 1831* Usage: *National and Civil*

Black is taken from the shield of the arms

Red is adapted from the lions claws and tongue

The vertical layout is derived from the French Tricolore

Gold is the colour of the lion in the arms

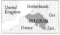
FOLLOWING CENTURIES of foreign domination, Belgium finally gained international recognition as an independent kingdom in 1830.

Black, yellow and red have been the colours of Belgium since before independence. They were derived from the coat of arms of Brabant which depicts a black shield and a gold lion with red tongue and claws. The first flag in these colours was raised in 1792, during an attempt to gain Belgian independence from Austria, but the stripes were then horizontal. They were changed to the vertical position, after independence in 1831, in imitation of the French *Tricolore*, which represented liberty and revolution. They have remained unchanged ever since.

Belgian Regional flags

BRUSSELS

Adopted in 1991, the lily was widespread in the area which later became Brussels.

FLANDERS

Adopted in 1985, it is based on the arms, and the colours are taken from the national flag.

WALLONIA

The cockerel is derived from the Gallic cock, recalling the cultural links with France.

IRELAND

Ratio: 1:2 Adopted: *21 January 1919* Usage: *National and Civil*

Green represents the Catholic people

Orange is for the Protestant people

White is for the union between Catholics and Protestants

AFTER CENTURIES of British rule, Ireland was split in 1921, becoming the Free State (The Republic of Ireland) and the northern Six Counties.

The Irish flag is modelled on that of the French *Tricolore*. It was first flown by nationalists during their struggle for freedom from Britain in 1848, a year of Europe-wide revolution. But it was not until the Easter Rising of 1916 that it came to be regarded as the national flag. It was officially confirmed in 1919 and was written into the Constitution in 1937. The green colouring on the flag represents the Catholic majority; orange is for the Protestant minority (originally supporters of William of Orange) and white is for peace between the two faiths.

THE PRESIDENT'S STANDARD

The flag of the President was introduced in 1945 and is based on the ancient 'Green Flag', a traditional symbol of Irish nationalism.

THE PRESIDENT'S STANDARD

The harp is said to be the harp of Brian Boru, an 11th century ruler

The flag is similar to the quartering for Ireland on the Royal Arms of the United Kingdom

UNITED KINGDOM

Ratio: *1:2*   Adopted: *1 January 1801*   Usage: *National and Civil*

The white saltire on a blue field was taken from the St Andrew's Cross

The saltire of St Patrick has been counter-changed with the white saltire of St Andrew

The central red cross, fimbriated with white was adapted from the St George's Cross

EUROPE

THE UNITED KINGDOM was formed in 1707, uniting England, Scotland and Wales. In 1801 Ireland joined, but in 1921 the south broke away.

The Union Flag is probably one of the world's best known flags, partially due to its unusual design, but more importantly, because of the importance of the British Empire in World history.

THE FIRST UNION FLAG
When King James of Scotland became King of England in 1603, both countries retained their own flags. Even today, the St George's Cross and St Andrew's Cross remain the flags of England and Scotland respectively. In 1606 King James considered it necessary to have a flag reflecting the new union of Scotland and England and ordered that a Union Flag, more commonly known

as the Union Jack, be flown on British ships, combining the English Cross of St George with the Scottish Cross of St Andrew.

A NEW UNION FLAG
In 1801, when Ireland joined the Union, the so-called Cross of St Patrick was added to form the present flag, but was counterchanged with the Cross of St Andrew.

A ROYAL FLAG
The Union Flag was established as a maritime flag and it remains a royal flag, not officially a national flag. The right of British citizens to fly the Union Jack on land must still be granted by royal permission.

UK – *Subnational flags*

MOST REGIONAL FLAGS are older than the Union Flag, except those based on the St George's Cross, which date from the 20th century.

 ENGLAND

Originally used in 1191, the flag of St George became the flag of England after 1277. The white flag has a red upright cross throughout. At sea it is the flag of an Admiral.

 WALES

Approved in 1959 as the Welsh national flag, the Red Dragon is an ancient emblem of Wales. For a time it appeared on a green hill, but the horizontal division is traditional.

 SCOTLAND
(The Standard)

The red lion on gold is the traditional royal flag of Scotland. The *fleur-de-lis* on the border recall the 'auld alliance' with France. Its exact date of adoption is not known.

 SCOTLAND
(National flag)

In use since 1512, the Scottish flag is the Cross of St Andrew. As James was King of Scotland before he was King of England, this flag formed the basis of the Union Flag.

 ISLE OF MAN

Again this is a traditional design. It was adopted in 1968. The *Trinacria*, three legs of Man, has been used for several centuries in varying forms, but its origin is uncertain.

 GUERNSEY

Guernsey formerly used only the Cross of St George. In 1985 a gold cross taken from the flag of William the Conqueror at the Battle of Hastings was added to the flag.

 JERSEY

Prior to the adoption of its current flag, Jersey used a red diagonal cross on white, which is the same as the saltire of St Patrick. The arms were added in 1981.

UK – Royal Standards

LIKE OTHER MONARCHIES, the UK has a wide range of flags which are armorial or semi-armorial, for the leading members of its royal family. In the case of HM Queen it is necessary to distinguish between her role as Queen of the United Kingdom and her other Realms, and as Head of the Commonwealth. In addition to her British Royal Standard she has standards for other Realms.

ROYAL STANDARD OF THE UNITED KINGDOM

This form has been in use since the accession of Queen Victoria in 1837 and depicts the three areas united to form the United Kingdom (England, Scotland and Ireland). Strictly, flags of this kind are armorial banners rather than 'standards'.

QUEEN AS HEAD OF THE COMMONWEALTH

This is used when the Queen is not in a 'Queen's Realm' (i.e. a country of which she is directly the Head of State) or in one which does not have a local Royal Standard. It is a banner with Her Majesty's initial 'E', a gold crown and chaplet of roses.

PRINCE PHILIP DUKE OF EDINBURGH

The banner for Prince Philip has quarters representing his descent from the royal families of both Denmark and Greece, and from the Mountbattens, and his title Duke of Edinburgh is represented by the arms of the city.

HRH PRINCE CHARLES

The banner is an adaptation of the Royal Standard, with a 'label' for an eldest son; a white bar with three points, and the quartered arms of the Principality of Wales over all in the centre. Labels are used for children and grandchildren of the Queen.

HRH PRINCE CHARLES FOR USE IN WALES

For personal visits to Wales and as his own flag, the Prince uses the banner of the Principality of Wales with his crown on a green shield over all in the centre. The Prince also has banners for his titles in Cornwall, Rothesay and as Lord of the Isles.

OTHER ROYAL STANDARDS

Other members who have standards based on the Royal Standard are the Queen Mother, the Princess Royal, Princess Margaret, the Duke of York, Prince Edward and the Queen's royal cousins. There is a general banner for those members of the royal family not entitled to an individual standard.

UK – Overseas Territories

OFFICIAL FLAGS for British Overseas Territories are generally based on the British blue or government ensign with a local badge in the fly.

 ANGUILLA

The flag of Anguilla was adopted in 1990. It is a blue ensign with the badge of the island. This derives from the unofficial flag used locally on land only.

 ANGUILLA (Unofficial)

Adopted in 1967, when the island separated from St Kitts and Nevis. The turquoise stripe represents the sea, and the three dolphins are for friendship, wisdom and strength.

 BERMUDA

Unusually, Bermuda uses a red ensign. The badge shows a lion holding a shield on which appears the 1609 wreck of a ship, which struck a reef, not a cliff as is shown.

 BRITISH VIRGIN ISLANDS

The badge dates from 1909, the flag from 1956. It shows St Ursula, the namesake of the islands, with a lamp. She was martyred with 11,000 virgins, represented by 11 lamps.

 BRITISH ANTARCTIC TERRITORY

The badge is white for the Antarctic ice and snow, with wavy blue lines for the sea. The torch shows the quest for knowledge. It was adopted in 1962 and is used on research ships.

 BRITISH INDIAN OCEAN TERRITORY

The flag was adopted in 1990. Blue and white wavy lines represent the ocean and the palm recalls the natural vegetation of the islands. The crown shows British possession.

 CAYMAN ISLANDS

Blue and white lines recall the sea and the three stars, the three main islands. The lion of England appears above and the crest is a turtle and a pineapple for the fauna and flora.

 FALKLAND ISLANDS

The badge shows a ram for the sheep industry of the islands. The ship is the *Desire*, the ship of John Davies who discovered the islands in 1592. The flag was hoisted in 1948.

GIBRALTAR
(Ensign)

GIBRALTAR
(City)

The blue ensign of Gibraltar was officially adopted in 1895. The badge is based on the arms of Gibraltar granted by Ferdinand, the King of Spain in 1502. The castle and key recall that Gibraltar is both a fortress and, because of its position on one side of a narrow strait, also the key to the Mediterranean Sea.

The local flag of Gibraltar City is a banner of the arms officially granted in 1926. It is based on the original arms granted by Spain in 1502. The banner was granted for use exclusively on land in 1983. Like the badge it depicts a red fortress with a gold key. The red and white field is derived from the arms.

MONTSERRAT

PITCAIRN
ISLANDS

The coat of arms dates from 1909, although its origin is unknown. It shows a woman in green holding a cross and a harp. The cross is for Christianity and the woman and harp recall Irish immigrants who settled on the island in 1632. The arms were re-adopted in 1962 when the West Indies Federation was dissolved.

Adopted for the Pitcairn Islands in 1984, the badge commemorates the island's earliest settlers, the infamous crew of the HMS *Bounty*, who mutinied in 1790. The badge is blue to represent the Pacific Ocean, with a green triangle symbolizing the island. The shield is charged with the Bible and the anchor of HMS *Bounty*.

ST HELENA

TURKS AND
CAICOS
ISLANDS

The current badge was made into a coat of arms in 1984. It depicts a ship flying the Cross of St George sailing between two cliffs. Above is a wire-bird representing the local fauna. The flag is also flown in the Ascension Islands and Tristan da Cunha, dependencies administered by St Helena.

The blue ensign was granted in 1968, three years after the arms. The shield from the arms shows a conch-shell and a crayfish representing fishing, the islands' main industry, and a cactus for their flora. The Turks and Caicos became a separate colony after the Bahamas achieved independence.

FRANCE

Ratio: 2:3   Adopted: *15 February 1794*   Usage: *National and Civil*

Red, white and blue have come to represent liberty, equality and fraternity – the ideals of the French Revolution

Blue and red are the colours of Paris

White is the colour of the House of Bourbon

EUROPE

FRANCE WAS A MONARCHY until the the Revolution of 1789. A republic was created in 1792, following the abolition of the monarchy.

The traditional emblem of France was the *fleur-de-lis*, or lily, which first appeared on the arms in the 12th century.

A REVOLUTIONARY FLAG
The *Tricolore* was used during the Revolution and has since become a symbol of liberty around the world.

Other nations have also adopted the design. Because France has no arms, the *Tricolore* is also the national emblem.

The colours are probably derived from those of Paris, combined with those of the Bourbon Dynasty, though they are usually associated with liberty, equality and fraternity.

Overseas Territories

CORSICA

Corsica flies an heraldic flag featuring a black Saracen's head on a white field. It is the emblem of the Corsican separatists.

FRENCH POLYNESIA

Red and white are local colours. The emblem depicts a *pirogue* – a local canoe – below a rising sun. The five crew recall the five island groups.

LUXEMBOURG

Ratio: 3:5   Adopted: *1848*   Usage: *National*

The blue stripe is paler than that of the Netherlands

The colours date back to the 13th century

EUROPE

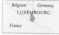

FOR MOST OF THE 19TH CENTURY Luxembourg was part of the Netherlands. It gained independence in 1890 and is Europe's last independent duchy.

Luxembourg had no flag until 1830, when patriots were urged to display the national colours. The flag was defined as a horizontal tricolour of red, white and blue in 1848, but it was not officially adopted until 1972. The tricolour flag is almost identical to that of the Netherlands, except that it is longer and its blue stripe is a lighter shade. The red, white and blue colouring was derived from the Grand Duke's coat of arms, which dates from the 13th century.

THE CIVIL ENSIGN
Since 1972 a banner of the Grand Duke's arms has been used as a civil ensign for use at sea. This is a blue and white-striped field with a lion rampant in the centre.

LUXEMBOURG CIVIL ENSIGN

Red, white and blue colouring gave rise to colours of national flag

A crowned two-tailed lion rampant

MONACO

Ratio: 4:5   Adopted: *4 April 1881*   Usage: *National and Civil*

The bicolour design is common on other national flags, for example San Marino. It is often used as a background for heraldic livery

Red and white are the heraldic colours of the Grimaldi family

EUROPE

THE GRIMALDIS, a Genoese family, have ruled Monaco since the 13th century. Until 1860, the principality was considered part of Italy.

The present bicolour design was adopted in 1881 under Prince Charles III. It is identical to the far younger Indonesian national flag except in its statutory proportions which are 4:5, compared to 2:3.

The Grimaldi coat of arms, which appears on the state flag, is the traditional one of the princely family and consists of a shield supported by two monks bearing swords. The device alludes to the legend of 1297, in which the Grimaldis conquered Monaco after entering the city with soldiers disguised as monks. Earlier Monegasque flags incorporated the Grimaldi shield and crown on a white field.

ARMS OF GRIMALDIS

A princely crown

The collar of the Order of St Charles surrounds a shield of red and white (or silver)

The Grimaldi motto – Deo Juvante ('With God's Help')

ANDORRA

Ratio: 2:3   Adopted: c 1866   Usage: National

The colours reflect Andorra's dependence upon France and Spain

Red and yellow are taken from the colours of Spain

Andorran coat of arms

Blue and red are taken from the colours of France

EUROPE

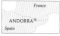

France

ANDORRA

Spain

THE PRINCIPALITY OF ANDORRA is an independent republic in the Pyrenees, between France and Spain. It is one of the world's oldest states.

The principality of Andorra has been under Franco-Spanish protection since 1278, governed by the Counts of Foix and the Bishops of Urgel. The colours of its national flag reflect both France: blue and red; and Spain: yellow and red. The Andorran coat of arms is placed in the middle of the yellow stripe.

ARMS OF ANDORRA
Like the colours of the flag, the coat of arms also depicts the areas on which Andorra has been dependent. The quartered shield represents Urgel by the crozier and mitre, Foix by the three vertical red stripes, Catalonia by the four vertical red stripes and Béarn by the two cows.

ARMS OF ANDORRA

The crozier and mitre symbolize the Bishops of Urgel

The four red stripes are taken from the arms of Catalonia

VIRTVS VNITA FORTIOR

The three red stripes recall the Counts of Foix

The two cows are taken from the arms of Béarn

The motto is, 'Virtus Unita Fortior' – 'Strength united is stronger'

PORTUGAL

Ratio: 2:3 Adopted: *30 June 1911* Usage: *National and Civil*

The armillary sphere – an early navigational tool

Red represents revolution

Green represents a Portuguese explorer; King Henry the Navigator

EUROPE

France

PORTUGAL Spain

DURING THE 15th and 16th centuries, Portugal played a leading role in discovering the world beyond Europe. It formed a republic in 1910.

With the republic, came a new flag. Portugal's old blue and white flag was replaced by a red and green one, representing revolution in red and Portuguese exploration in green.

AN IMPERIAL PAST

The central emblem symbolizes episodes from Portugal's imperial past. The white shield recalls King Alphonso Henriques, who established Portugal as an independent kingdom. The seven gold castles stand for Portugal's expansion as a result of Alphonso's marriage in 1146. Behind the shield is an armillary sphere, which was an early navigational tool.

EMBLEM OF PORTUGAL

This armillary sphere and shields appear in the centre of the Portuguese coat of arms

The seven gold castles stand for Portuguese expansion

The armillary sphere recalls the importance of Portuguese exploration of the globe

The blue shields represent King Alphonso Henriques

SPAIN

Ratio: 2:3   Adopted: *19 July 1927*   Usage: *National and Civil*

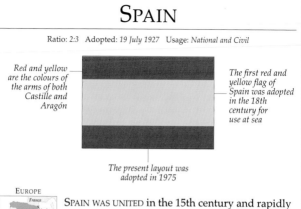

Red and yellow are the colours of the arms of both Castille and Aragón

The first red and yellow flag of Spain was adopted in the 18th century for use at sea

The present layout was adopted in 1975

EUROPE

SPAIN WAS UNITED in the 15th century and rapidly became an imperial power. It lost most of its colonies during the 19th century.

Early Spanish flags were mostly heraldic; some, like the flag of Castilla y León *(see page 140)* survive today.

In 1785 the King of Spain adopted the red and yellow to distinguish his ships from those of other countries. The combination of colours was used by no other country and although the present design was not adopted until 1927, they have always been associated with Spain. The colours were taken from the red and gold arms of both Castille and Aragón, the two regions united by King Ferdinand and Queen Isabella.

THE SPANISH REPUBLIC

When Spain became a republic in 1931, a new flag was adopted. This was an equal horizontal tricolour of red, yellow and purple. The purple is thought to have referred to either the arms of León or Granada. However when General Franco overthrew the republic in 1939, the original colours were restored.

THE NATIONAL ARMS

For state purposes the flag has the national arms set towards the hoist. The arms reflects the regions of Spain. The first and fourth quarters of the shield combine quarters representing Castille and León. The others recall Aragón and Navarre. In the base is the pomegranate of Granada. The whole shield is supported by the Pillar of Hercules.

Spain – Regional flags

ALTHOUGH MOST OF THE flags were adopted recently, all are based on older models, or traditional arms, displaying continuity with the past.

 ANDALUSIA

Adopted in 1918, but not confirmed until 1983, the colours were those used during the Napoleonic Wars. The coat of arms depicts the Pillars of Hercules and the lions of Cadiz.

 ARAGÓN

The stripes of Aragón date from the 14th century. Tradition states that a King of Aragón drew bloodstained fingers over a gold shield. The flag was adopted in 1981.

 ASTURIAS

Blue is the colour of the Virgin Mary. The cross is the Cross of Victory, a traditional Asturian emblem. From it hang Greek letters, symbolizing Christ, the Beginning, and the End.

 BALEARES

The field is the same as the flag of Aragón, to which the islands belonged in medieval times. The canton is the emblem of Palma de Majorca, the islands' capital.

THE BASQUE COUNTRY
(PAÍS VASCO)

This flag was first adopted in 1931 and re-adopted in 1979. It is based on the Union Jack. Red recalls bloodshed, white the Catholic faith, and green the Oak of Guérnica.

 CANARY ISLANDS
(ISLAS CANARIAS)

The colours symbolize those of the Virgin Mary and the Papacy. They are also thought to evoke the blue sea, the white beaches and the golden sun.

 CANTABRIA

White and red are the traditional colours of the area. The arms allude to the seafaring customs of the people and include an ancient seal. The flag was adopted in 1981.

 CASTILLA-LA MANCHA

Adopted in 1989, the red stripe and the castle are the emblem of Castile. The white panel is intended to recall the surcoats worn by the soldiers in the Crusades.

CASTILLA Y LEÓN

This flag has been used by Castilla y León since 1248. It depicts the union of Castilla (castle) and León (lion). It was adopted for the region in 1989.

 CATALONIA (*CATALUNYA*)

The flag, adopted in 1932, has been used since the 13th century and has the same origin as that of Aragón. It was outlawed from 1939 to 1975.

 EXTREMADURA

This flag was adopted in 1985, but the colours are traditional regional colours. Green is for fidelity, white for truth and black for courage.

 GALICIA

Based on a traditional Galician design, white and blue are the colours of the Virgin Mary. The arms reflects loyalty to the Catholic Church.

 LA RIOJA

The upper red stripe was originally to be in the colour of Rioja wine, but is now simply red. The colours are taken from the arms.

 MADRID

The flag, adopted in 1983, is in the traditional colour of Castilla. The seven white stars, from the arms, are for the seven districts of the region.

 MURCIA

The four castles recall Murcia's links with Castilla and the seven crowns, the seven regions of the province.

 NAVARRE

The red field and golden chains of Navarre date from the 14th century. The current flag was adopted in 1982.

 VALENCIA

The stripes recall Valencia's links with Catalonia and the stylized crown, its period of independence.

ITALY

Ratio: 2:3 Adopted: *18 June 1946* Usage: *National*

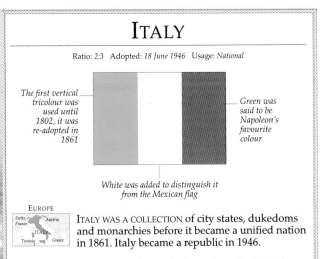

The first vertical tricolour was used until 1802, it was re-adopted in 1861

Green was said to be Napoleon's favourite colour

White was added to distinguish it from the Mexican flag

EUROPE

ITALY WAS A COLLECTION of city states, dukedoms and monarchies before it became a unified nation in 1861. Italy became a republic in 1946.

The Italian tricolour comes from the standard designed by Napoleon during the Italian campaign of 1796. The colouring was influenced by the French *Tricolore*, at first appearing in horizontal bands. The vertical tricolour was introduced in 1798, but was only used until the fall of Napoleon in 1814. It was re-introduced when the new Kingdom of Italy was formed in 1861. When the monarchy ended in 1946, the coat of arms of the House of Savoy was removed from the flag. The present flag was officially adopted in 1946.

ITALIAN CIVIL ENSIGN

The most famous seafaring states of ancient Italy are commemorated in the quarters of the civil ensign.

ITALIAN CIVIL ENSIGN

The winged lion of St Mark represents Venice

The Maltese cross recalls Amalfi

The Cross of St George represents Genoa

The Pisan cross stands for Pisa

MALTA

Ratio: 2:3   Adopted: *21 September 1964*   Usage: *National*

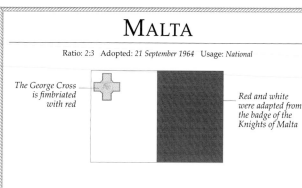

The George Cross is fimbriated with red

Red and white were adapted from the badge of the Knights of Malta

MALTA WAS RULED successively by the Knights of St John of Jerusalem, by Napoleon and by Britain. It became independent in 1964.

A key stronghold during the Crusades, much of the heraldry of Malta is influenced by the colours and devices of the Knights of Malta. Their badge was the characteristic Maltese cross and their arms was a white cross on a red field. From these colours came the red and white shield that was used during the colonial period. The George Cross

medal was added to the shield in 1943. It was awarded to the islanders by King George VI of Britain for heroism in the Second World War. In 1964, the blue canton on which the cross was originally placed was replaced by a red fimbriation.

The President's flag, introduced in 1988, has the shield on a blue field, with a Maltese cross in each corner.

THE PRESIDENT'S FLAG

The wreath of olive and palm branches represents peace

A gold mural crown with a sally port and eight turrets represents fortifications of Valetta

The Maltese cross

The Shield of Malta

VATICAN CITY

Ratio: 1:1   Adopted: 7 June 1929   Usage: Civil

Yellow (gold) and white (silver) are the colours of St Peter's keys

The emblem features St Peter's keys supporting the papal crown

Yellow and white were adopted as the papal colours in 1808

EUROPE

Italy
VATICAN CITY

VATICAN CITY, the Holy See of the Roman Catholic Church, is the smallest independent state in the world.

The modern Vatican colours were first adopted as the papal colours in 1808. The flag was used until 1870 when the Papal States were incorporated into a new unified Italy. In 1929, the Papal States were granted independent status, but their authority was confined to Vatican City. Gold and silver, represented in the flag as yellow and white, are the colours of the keys of St Peter, which have accompanied papal arms since the Middle Ages. The flag's white stripe bears an emblem used since the 13th century to represent the Vatican's role as the headquarters of the Roman Catholic Church.

EMBLEM OF VATICAN CITY

The triple crown signifies the three types of temporal power – legislative, executive and judicial – vested in the Pope

The crossed keys represent the keys to the Kingdom of Heaven bestowed by Christ on St Peter

A red ropes binds the keys

SAN MARINO

Ratio: 4:5   Adopted: 6 April 1862   Usage: National and Civil

White represents the snow on Mt Titano and the clouds above it

The colours are taken from the traditional arms, which is placed at the centre of the flag for official purposes only

Blue recalls the sky

EUROPE

FOUNDED IN THE 4TH CENTURY, the Republic of San Marino is one of the smallest and oldest in the world. It lies on the slopes of Mt Titano in Italy.

The flag of San Marino dates back to 1797 and was recognized by Napoleon as that of an independent state in 1799. The colours were taken from the coat of arms and were introduced in the 18th century. Blue is said to represent the sky over San Marino and white the clouds and snow on Mt Titano.

The traditional coat of arms is placed in the centre of the flag for official purposes only. It depicts three white towers crowned with ostrich plumes, representing three citadels resting on the peak of Mt Titano, which was once vaned with ostrich feathers. They symbolize the state's ability to defend itself.

ARMS OF SAN MARINO

A wreath of laurel

The towers represent the three citadels, Guaita, Cesta and Montale, situated on Mt Titano

A wreath of oak

The motto 'Libertas', meaning 'Liberty', also dates back to the 4th century, when the state was established as a refuge for those fleeing religious persecution

SWITZERLAND

Ratio: *1:1*   Adopted: *12 December 1889*   Usage: *National and Civil*

The red field with a white cross was adapted from the flag of Schwyz, one of the original three cantons

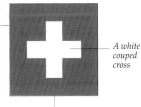

A white coupled cross

This is the only square national flag (apart from that of the Vatican)

IN 1291, A SMALL CONFEDERATION was formed to resist Austrian rule, beginning modern Switzerland. More cantons joined up to 1815.

The flag of Switzerland is one of the most typical European flags. In medieval times many European states used a plain flag with a cross.

A FLAG FOR THE CONFEDERATION
For many years, the separate cantons of Switzerland had no one common flag, but were each represented by their own flags. The present flag of Switzerland, a white coupled cross on a red field, was based on that of Schwyz, one of the three original provinces which united into a confederation against the Holy Roman Empire in 1291. It became accepted as the common badge of the Confederation in 1339 at the Battle of Laupen, when it was used

to distinguish the soldiers of the Confederation from other soldiers, and became the accepted flag of the Confederation in 1480. It was not officially confirmed as the flag of Switzerland until 1848 and it was last regulated in 1889.

Apart from that of the Vatican, the Swiss flag is the only totally square national flag. However, when used on the Swiss lakes it has the ratio of 2:3; a practice adopted in 1941.

THE NATIONAL ARMS
The coat of arms is simply a shield in the form of the flag. It was officially adopted in 1889. Every town or commune in Switzerland has its own flag and coat of arms.

Switzerland – Canton flags

IN EVERY CASE the flags are based on the arms of the canton, some of which predate the canton's joining the Swiss Confederation.

 AARGAU

Adopted in 1803, the white waves on black represent the River Aare, and the white stars on blue, the districts of Baden, the Free Areas and Fricktal which came together to form the canton. In 1963 it was decreed that the stars should be arranged 2 and 1.

 APPENZELL AUSSER-RHODEN

Adopted in 1597 when the canton separated from the Inner-Rhoden, the flag retained the bear, but added the initials VR (for Ussroden). The bear dates back to medieval banners. It was used from 1403 in battles against feudal landlords.

 APPENZELL INNER-RHODEN

This is the original form of the flag before the partition from Appenzell Ausser-Rhoden in 1597. The bear emblem was widely used locally in the Middle Ages, and was taken by the Appenzellers from the arms of the abbey of Sankt Gallen.

 BASEL-LAND

Basel-Land separated from the City in 1832. The arms and flag were adopted in 1834 based on the form of crozier used in Liestal, with the crook turned to the right and decorated with small spheres. This was made official in 1947.

 BASEL-STADT

The emblem of Basel-Stadt is the headpiece of a bishop's crozier. The emblem dates back to the earliest days of heraldry. Since the 15th century it has been depicted as black on white. It was kept in this form when the canton was divided in 1832.

 BERN

The coat of arms dates back to the 12th century. Soon after which the arms, which depict a bear on a red field with a yellow diagonal, became the canton's banner. There have, however, been many variant forms through the ages. The bear represents the name of the canton.

FRIBOURG

The original colours of Fribourg, black and white, were re-adopted when it joined the Confederation in 1831, but date back to 1410 and are related to the coat of arms.

GENEVA

The eagle recalls the former Holy Roman Empire. The key is the Key of St Peter, and shows Geneva as the key to western Switzerland. The flag was adopted in 1815.

GLARUS

The flag of Glarus depicts the figure of St Fridolin, the patron saint of the canton, on a red field. The flag was adopted when the canton joined the Confederation in 1352.

GRAUBUNDEN

The flag includes symbols for the three original parts of the canton which united in the 15th century: Graubunden, Zehgerichtenbund and the Gotteshausbund.

JURA

This flag was adopted 1978, when Jura became a separate canton. It was formerly part of Basel-Land – recalled by the crozier – and Bern. The stripes are from the arms of Jura.

LUCERNE

Lucerne was the first canton, after the original three, to join the Confederation in 1332. Its flag has the colours of its shield arranged horizontally instead of vertically.

NEUCHÂTEL

The tricolour adopted in 1848 is in traditional colours. The white cross was added to show the canton's association with Switzerland.

NIDWALDEN

The key with two wards is the emblem of St Peter, and was used in the 15th century. It was retained when the canton divided in 1815.

OBWALDEN

The key with only one ward was used in Obwalden from the 13th century and it was this form that was adopted when the separate canton was formed in 1815.

SANKT GALLEN

The emblems of Sankt Gallen – an axe and a fasces – were adopted in 1803 when the canton was formed under French influence. They are both symbols of republicanism.

SCHAFFHAUSEN

The emblem has been in use since the 14th century. It depicts a ram (the 'sheep' of the town's name) on a yellow field. The flag's existence was first recorded as early as 1386.

SCHWYZ

Schwyz was one of the first three cantons, and the one from which the country takes its name. Its arms existed before the Confederation was formed in 1291.

SOLOTHURN

The coat of arms dates back to 1394 and has colours derived from those of the Confederation. The flag was originally red with a white cross, but was simplified into its current form.

THURGAU

The flag of Thurgau, adopted in 1803, depicts two gold lions arranged diagonally. They are taken from the coat of arms which dates from medieval times.

TICINO

The colours of Ticino's flag may be derived from the French *Tricolore*, or from the main colours of the arms of the united townships.

URI

The emblem is an auroch's head (linked to the canton's name). It dates from the 13th century, but the nose-ring was added later.

VALAIS

The modern flag of Valais is derived from that of the original republic, which had seven stars for its component townships. These were increased to 12 in 1802 and retained when the state joined the Confederation in 1814.

 VAUD

The colours date from 1798 when the Léman Republic was formed, and stand for freedom. They were retained when the state entered the Confederation in 1803. The motto is '*Liberté et Patrie*' ('Freedom and Fatherland').

ZUG

Zug joined the Confederation in 1352 and again in 1364, after a brief return to Habsburg rule. The colours of the flag were originally red-white-red of Austria, but were altered to the blue and white from the arms of the Counts of Lenzburg in 1352.

 ZÜRICH

The flag in this case preceded the arms and dates back to the 13th century. It was adopted in 1351 when Zürich joined the Confederation. However since 1957 it has been compulsory to depict the flag in the same format as the shield.

LIECHTENSTEIN

Ratio: 3:5   Adopted: *24 June 1937*   Usage: *National and Civil*

The yellow crown was introduced to distinguish Liechtenstein as a principality

Red and royal blue have been used to represent the country of Liechtenstein since the 18th century

EUROPE

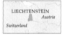

THE PRINCIPALITY OF LIECHTENSTEIN was created in 1719 as part of the Holy Roman Empire. It gained full independence in 1806.

The red and blue of Liechtenstein's flag date from 1921. There was confusion at the 1936 Olympic Games in Berlin because the flag was very similar to that of Haiti. In 1937 the crown was introduced to the flag of Liechtenstein to establish the country's status as a principality and to distinguish it from the Haitian flag. The flag can be hung vertically or horizontally, but the crown always remains upright.

THE PRINCE'S FLAG

The arms of Silesia, Künringen, Troppau and East Friesland and Rietburg make up the four quarters of the shield of the Prince's arms, in the centre of his flag. They represent the noble ancestors of the prince.

THE FLAG OF PRINCE OF LIECHTENSTEIN

The inner shield represents the ancient princely family

Red and yellow are the Prince's colours

The four arms within the Prince's Arms represent his noble ancestors

AUSTRIA

Ratio: 2:3   Adopted: *1 May 1945*   Usage: *National and Civil*

According to legend, the red and white flag was modelled on the blood-stained surcoat of a Duke wounded in battle

The traditional flag, retained after the fall of the Habsburgs in 1918

AUSTRIA ONCE RULED much of central Europe, but lost most of its territory in 1919. Between 1938 and 1945 Austria was annexed to Germany.

Tradition states that a Duke of Austria once fought so fiercely in battle that the white surcoat he wore was soaked in blood, except for the part covered by his sword-belt. So he adopted red with a white band across the centre as his colours.

ONE OF THE WORLD'S OLDEST FLAGS

The story is probably apocryphal, but stripes of red-white-red have been an emblem of Austria for over 800 years. Their use on a flag was recorded in 1191, making the Austrian flag one of the world's oldest flags. It was officially adopted as the national flag after the fall of the Habsburg Dynasty, and the formation of a republic in 1918.

During the Second World War, the Austrian flag and arms were banned, they were restored in 1945.

ARMS OF AUSTRIA

The coat of arms depicts an imperial black eagle, an emblem used by the Habsburgs. It originally had two heads, but they were changed to one when the Habsburg Empire disintegrated. On the eagle's chest is a shield in the national colours. The eagle holds a hammer and sickle recalling agricultural and industrial workers. Its crown, with three turrets, also represents agriculture, industry and commerce. The broken chains on the eagle's feet symbolize the restoration of freedom.

Austria – State flags

MOST PROVINCIAL FLAGS in Austria are based on the local arms. In many cases they existed before their official adoption.

 BURGENLAND

The colours of the flag, officially hoisted in 1971, are based on the red eagle and yellow shield of the arms.

 CARINTHIA

Adopted in 1946, the colours are derived from those of Austria and the yellow state shield.

 LOWER AUSTRIA

Adopted in 1954, the colours are based on the arms which contain a blue shield and five gold eagles.

 SALZBURG

The flag, adopted in 1921, uses the traditional colours of the state, based on the national colours.

 STYRIA

The coat of arms of Styria is a green shield bearing a white lion. The flag, adopted in 1960, uses these colours.

 TYROL

The bicoloured flag is derived from the arms which depicts a red eagle on a white disc. It was adopted in 1945.

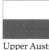 UPPER AUSTRIA

Upper Austria's flag, adopted in 1949, is derived from the national colours and the arms of the province.

 VIENNA

The flag dates from 1946. It is based on the city's arms, but is identical to the flags of Salzburg and Vorarlberg.

 VORARLBERG

Like the flags of Salzburg and Vienna, Vorarlberg's bicolour flag is based on the provincial arms.

HUNGARY

Ratio: 2:3 Adopted: 1 October 1957 Usage: National and Civil

Red symbolizes strength

White represents faithfulness

Green is symbolic of hope

PART OF AUSTRIA-HUNGARY until 1918, the nation became part of the communist bloc from 1945–1989.

The current flag was first used in the 1848–49 uprising. Its pattern was derived from the French *Tricolore* used during the French Revolution. The colours: red, white and green date back to the 9th century. They were first used in 1608 during the reign of King Matthias II. Until 1945, the royal crown featured in the centre of the national flag. During Hungary's brief period as a republic from 1945–1949 the royal crown was replaced by the 'Kossuth' coat of arms. When the Communists took power, they added a Soviet-style emblem to the flag. In 1990, the arms of the kingdom were re-adopted but they were not replaced on the flag.

ARMS OF HUNGARY

The crown of St Stephen, the first king of Hungary

The red and white stripes probably originated from Spain in the late 12th or early 13th century

The patriarchal cross was added to the Hungarian arms about 800 years ago

CZECH REPUBLIC

Ratio: 2:3   Adopted: *30 March 1920*   Usage: *National and Civil*

The blue triangle was added to distinguish the flag from that of Poland

White and red are the heraldic colours of Bohemia (any similarity to the pan-Slavic colours is coincidental)

Blue represents the state of Moravia

EUROPE

THE CZECH REPUBLIC was part of Austria until 1919, when it merged with Slovakia to form Czechoslovakia. The states separated in 1993.

The first flag of Czechoslovakia was based on the arms, and was white over red. This was identical to the flag of Poland, so a blue triangle was added at the hoist. The flag was banned by the Nazis in 1938 and a horizontal tricolour of white, red and blue was enforced. The original flag was restored in 1949.

THE NEW CZECH REPUBLIC
When the Czech Republic and Slovakia separated in 1993, the Czechs decided to keep their existing flag, recalling the two principal parts of the country.

The greater coat of arms depicts a quartered shield reflecting the regions of the Czech Republic.

GREATER ARMS OF THE CZECH REPUBLIC

The white lion on a red field is the traditional emblem of Bohemia

The black eagle on a yellow field is taken from the arms of Silesia

The red and white eagle on a blue field is from the arms of Moravia

The Bohemian arms are repeated to fill the shield

SLOVAKIA

Ratio: 2:3   Adopted: 1 September 1992   Usage: National and Civil

The arms of Slovakia

A version of this flag was first used in the 19th century

Red, white and blue are pan-Slavic colours

EUROPE

UNDER HUNGARIAN RULE until 1919, Slovakia then formed part of Czechoslovakia with the Czech Republic. The two states separated in 1993.

The first Slovak flags, used during the 19th century, were like the contemporary Russian flag, to whom they looked for aid in gaining independence. As Czechoslovakia, a red and white flag with a blue triangle was used. During the Second World War, Slovakia re-adopted the white, blue and red tricolour, with the arms in the centre.

THE PRESIDENT'S FLAG

ARMS OF SLOVAKIA
The arms uses colours of the early flags, a white patriarchal cross rising from blue mountains on a red shield.

At independence in 1993, the red, white and blue tricolour was retained as the national flag, but the arms was placed towards the hoist.

The President's flag has the arms, bordered by the national colours.

The flag is bordered by stripes in the national colours; red, blue and white

A patriarchal cross

A stylized image of Slovakia's mountains

Slovenia

Ratio: 1:2   Adopted: *24 June 1991*   Usage: *National and Civil*

The coat of arms was added in 1991 when Slovenia became independent

White, blue and red are pan-Slavic colours, popularized in the 19th century

The order of the tricolour is the same as the flag for Slovenia, when it was part of Yugoslavia

EUROPE

HISTORICALLY UNDER **Austrian rule, Slovenia formed part of Yugoslavia in 1919. It declared independence on 26 June 1991.**

Like Slovakia, Slovenia looked to Russia in the 19th century for assistance in gaining independence. For the same reason, the pan-Slavic tricolour of blue, white and red was adopted for Yugoslavia, with a gold fimbriated red star added by Tito in 1946. Slovenia also had its own flag within Yugoslavia, distinguished by the order of the stripes (white, blue, red). At independence Slovenia placed its arms in the upper hoist of this tricolour, to create a distinct national flag.

The arms depicts mountain peaks, above wavy blue lines symbolizing the sea coast. The stars are from the arms of the Duchy of Selje.

ARMS OF SLOVENIA

The three stars are from the arms of the former Duchy of Selje

The three mountain peaks represent the Triglav, part of the Alps

The wavy lines symbolize Slovenia's sea coast

CROATIA

Ratio: 1:2   Adopted: 22 December 1991   Usage: National and Civil

Red, white and blue are traditional Croatian colours

The tricolour charged with the coat of arms was first used during the Second World War

Arms of Croatia

EUROPE

FOR MUCH OF ITS existence, Croatia was under Austrian rule. It joined Yugoslavia in 1919, but declared independence on 25 June 1991.

While part of Yugoslavia, Croatia's flag was designed in the pan-Slavic colours, red, white and blue. These are also traditional Croatian colours used in the 19th century.

During the Second World War Croatia became a semi-independent state and added the arms of Croatia to the centre of its flag. Following the war, Croatia retained its tricolour but a gold-edged red star was placed in the centre by Tito. Before gaining independence, the present flag was adopted, based on the one used during the war.

The shield is in the red and white checks of Croatia. Above is a row of shields of its various territories.

ARMS OF CROATIA

The small shields at the top are taken from the arms of Croatia's regions

From left to right the shields represent the ancient arms of Croatia, Dubrovnik, Dalmatia, Istria and Slavonia

The red and white checks are traditional emblems of Croatia

BOSNIA & HERZEGOVINA

Ratio: 1:2   Adopted: 4 May 1992   Usage: National and Civil

The shield is from the arms of King Stephen Tvrtho, who ruled before the Turks

The fleur-de-lis *recalls family ties to the Anjous, the ruling dynasty in Hungary in the 14th century*

EUROPE

BOSNIA-HERZEGOVINA was under Turkish rule until it was ceded to Austria in 1878. From 1945 to 1992 it formed part of Yugoslavia.

As part of Yugoslavia, Bosnia-Herzegovina adopted the blue, white and red pan-Slavic tricolour. After the Second World War, it had its own flag within Yugoslavia. This was a red field with the Yugoslavian flag in the canton.

The current flag was adopted in 1991. It is charged with the shield from the arms of King Stephen Tvrtho who was king of Bosnia-Herzegovina 1376–1391.

THE BOSNIA-CROAT FEDERATION

In the unrest following the break up of former Yugoslavia, the Bosnians allied with the Croats, forming the Bosnian-Croat Federation in 1996. Their flag is a horizontal tricolour with the arms of the Federation.

BOSNIA-CROAT FEDERATION FLAG

The first quarter is green with a gold lily from the Tvrtho arms

Red and white checks are the Croatian emblem

The ten stars are for the ten cantons in the Federation

YUGOSLAVIA (SERBIA & MONTENEGRO)

Ratio: 1:2 Adopted: 27 April 1992 Usage: National and Civil

The order of the colours in the tricolour was only used for the national flag of Yugoslavia

Blue, white and red are pan-Slavic colours, adopted in the 19th century

EUROPE

RULED BY TURKEY and Austria, a number of states united in 1919 to form Yugoslavia. In 1991, several areas declared independence.

Prior to its formation in 1919, nearly all the regions of Yugoslavia used red, white and blue pan-Slavic flags. To distinguish the national flag of Yugoslavia, the order of the stripes was made blue, white and red, an arrangement not used by the other states. The plain flag was used for civil purposes on land and sea.

The state flag had the Royal Arms in the centre.

After the Second World War, Yugoslavia became a communist state under Marshall Tito, and the coat of arms was replaced by a gold-edged red 'Partisan Star'. After the break-up of the country in 1991, the star was removed.

Yugoslavian States

MONTENEGRO

The flag is identical to Serbia's, except for its shape. Prior to Montenegro joining Yugoslavia, its flag bore a Royal Cypher. From 1946–1992 both contained gold-edged red stars.

SERBIA

The pan-Slavic flag has historically been used in Serbia. It is also used, in parts of Bosnia and Croatia inhabited by Serbs.

ALBANIA

Ratio: 5:7   Adopted: *7 April 1992*   Usage: *National*

The Albanians call their country, Shapipëria, meaning 'land of the eagle'

The traditional heraldic Albanian flag first used in 1912 when independence was restored

ONCE PART OF the Byzantine Empire, Albania became a kingdom in 1912. From 1944 to 1991 it was a strict communist state.

The black eagle first appeared on the Albanian flag in the 15th century when Albania became part of the Byzantine Empire. According to legend, the Albanians are the descendants of the eagle. The red flag, with the eagle in the centre, was adopted in 1912, when independence was restored. Parts of the Italian arms were included on the flag after the invasion of 1939, but the original flag was restored in 1942.

In 1946, the flag changed again, to incorporate a gold-edged red star above the eagle, representing the communist regime. The star was removed in 1991, by order of the new multiparty government.

ARMS OF ALBANIA

The black eagle has been an emblem of Albania since the 15th century

The two-headed eagle first appeared on flags used during the struggle against Turkish occupation

MACEDONIA

Ratio: *1:2*   Adopted: *5 October 1995*   Usage: *National and Civil*

Red was the traditional colour of the Macedonian flag

The radiant sun was added in 1995 to replace the controversial 'Star of Vergina'

EUROPE

MACEDONIA WAS under Turkish rule for centuries. It united with Serbia in 1913 and became part of Yugoslavia. It declared independence in 1992.

As part of Yugoslavia, Macedonia was the only region not to use the pan-Slavic colours. Its flag was red with a gold-edged red star in the canton.

A CONTROVERSIAL NEW FLAG
At independence in 1992, Macedonia retained the red flag but added a gold star in a gold sun. This was soon changed to the Star of Vergina, an ancient Macedonian emblem from the tomb of Philip of Macedon, father of Alexander the Great. Greece objected to this, claiming the star as a Greek emblem. In 1995 the star was replaced by a radiant sun.

Macedonia's arms is similar in design to former Soviet emblems.

ARMS OF MACEDONIA

The star of socialism

Symmetrical wreaths of wheat

A radiant sun, also used on the national flag

BULGARIA

Ratio: 3:5   Adopted: *22 November 1990*   Usage: *National and Civil*

Before 1990 the white stripe contained the Bulgarian coat of arms

The green stripe replaced the blue of the Russian tricolour

Red and white were taken from the pan-Slavic colours

EUROPE

BULGARIA BECAME **independent in 1908 after 500 years of Ottoman rule. In 1990, the communist regime, in power since 1946, collapsed.**

While under Turkish rule, Bulgaria had no national flag. When it became a principality in 1878, a slight variation of the pan-Slavic colours, widely used during the independence movements of the late 19th century, was adopted. The horizontal arrangement of the tricolour was based on the Russian flag at the time, but for Bulgaria's national flag the central blue stripe was substituted by green.

THE PEOPLE'S REPUBLIC
No change was made to the flag during Bulgaria's period as an independent kingdom 1908–1946, but with the formation of the People's Republic in 1947, a coat of

arms was added in the white stripe near the hoist. This depicted a rampant lion, a red star representing communism, and later a cog-wheel symbolizing industrialization. The coat of arms was removed from the flag in 1990 because of its communist connotations. No arms now appear on the flag.

THE SYMBOLISM OF THE COLOURS
Although based on the pan-Slavic colours, the white band is said to represent a love of peace, and red, the valour of the people. The green stripe, substituted for the traditional pan-Slavic blue in 1878, was intended to represent the youthfulness of the emerging nation.

GREECE

Ratio: 2:3 Adopted: *1822* Usage: *National and Civil*

The cross in the canton represents Greek religious faith

Blue represents the sea and sky

The nine stripes represent the nine syllables in the cry 'Freedom or Death', uttered during the Greek war of independence

White reflects the purity of the Greek independence struggle

ONCE PART of the Ottoman Empire, Greece has seen periodic unrest since the Second War World. In 1974 it became a multiparty democracy.

The flag flown by Greece is in the same colours as the one which was raised following independence from the Ottoman Empire in the early 19th century. At various times since the 19th century Greece has used a plain white cross on a blue background as its naval flag, its land flag. Today the plain Cross Flag is preserved in the President's flag and in the canton of the blue and white striped national flag.

The shade of blue of the flag has also varied. Today it is the original light blue colour of 1822. It was altered in the 1970s and the blue was changed to a much darker, navy shade.

THE PRESIDENT'S FLAG

The original white cross on a blue field is retained in the President's flag and the national arms

The Cross Flag is surrounded by a wreath of laurels

ROMANIA

Ratio: 2:3   Adopted: 27 December 1989   Usage: National and Civil

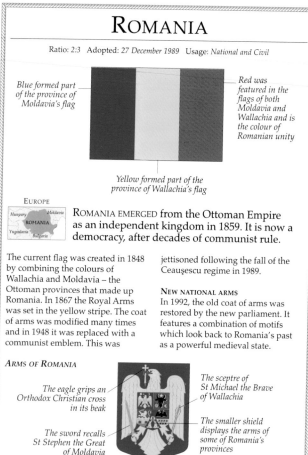

Blue formed part of the province of Moldavia's flag

Red was featured in the flags of both Moldavia and Wallachia and is the colour of Romanian unity

Yellow formed part of the province of Wallachia's flag

ROMANIA EMERGED from the Ottoman Empire as an independent kingdom in 1859. It is now a democracy, after decades of communist rule.

The current flag was created in 1848 by combining the colours of Wallachia and Moldavia – the Ottoman provinces that made up Romania. In 1867 the Royal Arms was set in the yellow stripe. The coat of arms was modified many times and in 1948 it was replaced with a communist emblem. This was jettisoned following the fall of the Ceauşescu regime in 1989.

NEW NATIONAL ARMS
In 1992, the old coat of arms was restored by the new parliament. It features a combination of motifs which look back to Romania's past as a powerful medieval state.

ARMS OF ROMANIA

The eagle grips an Orthodox Christian cross in its beak

The sword recalls St Stephen the Great of Moldavia

The sceptre of St Michael the Brave of Wallachia

The smaller shield displays the arms of some of Romania's provinces

MOLDAVIA

Ratio: 1:2   Adopted: 12 May 1990   Usage: National and Civil

The arms of
Moldavia

The blue, yellow and red colours
reflect strong links with Romania

EUROPE

MOLDAVIA WAS ONCE part of Romania, but was
incorporated into the Soviet Union in 1940. It has
been fully independent since 1991.

The blue, red and yellow tricolour of
Moldavia is almost identical the
Romanian flag, reflecting the two
countries' cultural affinity.

ARMS OF MOLDAVIA
On Moldavia's flag the yellow stripe
is charged with the national arms.
Like the Romanian coat of arms, the

Moldavian arms, adopted in 1990,
features a golden eagle holding an
Orthodox Christian cross in its beak.
However instead of a sword, the
eagle is holding an olive branch. The
blue and red shield on the eagle's
breast is also different – on it are an
ox-head, a star, a rose and a crescent,
all traditional symbols of Moldavia.

ARMS OF MOLDAVIA

An eagle holds an
Orthodox cross,
similar to that in the
arms of Romania

A star

An ox-head

A rose

A crescent

An olive branch
symbolizing peace

BELORUSSIA

Ratio: *1:2* Adopted: *16 May 1995* Usage: *National and Civil*

A national ornament representing woven cloth

Red and green were the colours of Belorussia's flag while it was a Soviet republic

Red and white are traditional Belorussian colours

EUROPE

BELORUSSIA, formerly White Russia, became independent of the USSR in 1991, although its ties with Russia are increasing once more.

The original flag of Belorussia while under Soviet administration in 1922 was similar to that of the USSR. It was changed in 1951, and the flag used today is similar to this second flag, except that the communist hammer, sickle and star have been removed, and the red and white portions of the hoist ornamentation have been reversed.

THE REJECTED DESIGN

Following independence from the USSR in 1991, Belorussia adopted a flag of three equal horizontal stripes of white-red-white. This was the same flag which had been associated with a brief period of Belorussian independence in 1918 and its colours

were derived from the arms of the republic. The design was rejected in a referendum in 1995.

The flag of Belorussia adopted following the referendum, reflects its growing ties with Russia. The unusual ornamentation in the hoist is described as a national ornament and represents woven cloth.

ARMS OF BELORUSSIA

The Soviet-style coat of arms, retained on independence, also reflects the dominant Russian influence. This depicts an outline of the state against a sun rising from behind a globe. This is entirely surrounded by wreaths of wheat and flowers.

UKRAINE

Ratio: 2:3   Adopted: 4 September 1991   Usage: National and Civil

Originally the flag of the republic in 1918

Blue represents the sky

Yellow recalls the vast grain fields

UKRAINE FORMED an independent state in 1918, but came under Soviet control one year later and remained so until independence in 1991.

The bicoloured flag flown in Ukraine today was the official flag of the country in 1918 when Ukraine enjoyed a brief period of independence. With the invasion of the Red Army, the flag was suppressed until the German occupation of 1941–1944. After the war it was banned again by the Soviet Union. When Ukraine gained its independence in 1991 the country re-adopted its original flag. The blue is supposed to represent the sky and the yellow the vast fields of grain of the country's agriculture.

The Ukrainian coat of arms is in the national colours and features an ancient trident symbol.

ARMS OF UKRAINE

Blue and yellow are national colours

The trident of St Volodimir

The trident is an ancient symbol dating back to pre-Roman times

RUSSIAN FEDERATION

Ratio: 2:3   Adopted: *22 August 1991*   Usage: *National and Civil*

The colours of the flag were adapted from the original flag of the Netherlands

Since its official adoption in 1799, the Russian tricolour has had a major influence on other east European flags

White, blue and red are pan-Slavic colours

RUSSIA WAS FORMED in the 15th century and, by 1922, when the USSR was established, included much of Asia. The USSR collapsed in 1991.

At the end of the 17th century, Tsar Peter the Great of Russia visited western Europe. Following this visit he decided to adopt a variation of the Dutch flag as a civil ensign for Russian ships. This was a horizontal tricolour of white, blue and red. It was only officially recognized in 1799. Peter the Great also adopted a flag for the Russian navy, which was white with the blue diagonal Cross of St Andrew.

THE PAN-SLAVIC COLOURS

Both the colour and tricolour design of this first flag had a major influence on many of the flags of Eastern European nations during the 19th century, who looked to Russia for help in liberating them from foreign domination. They have since become known as the pan-Slavic colours.

THE HAMMER, SICKLE AND STAR

After the Russian Revolution of 1917, the Communists abolished all former flags and instead adopted the Red Flag as the flag of the Soviet Union. This contained a gold hammer and sickle, symbols of the proletariat and the peasants, under a gold-edged red star, to represent unity. As a Soviet republic, Russia used this flag with a vertical blue bar at the hoist.

When the Soviet Union collapsed in 1991, the former flags of Russia, including the white, blue and red tricolour were restored.

Russian Federation – Republic flags

UNLIKE MOST OTHER COUNTRIES, the flags of the Russian republics are all new, adopted since 1991.

 RESPUBLIKA ADYGEYA

Designed by a British traveller who helped resist annexation of the republic by Russia, the arrows are for resistance. Green is for agriculture and gold is for freedom.

 RESPUBLIKA ALTAY

Blue represents the cleanliness of the sky, mountains, rivers and lakes of Altay. White is for eternity, and to encourage the revival of love and harmony between the Altay people.

 RESPUBLIKA BASHKORTOSTAN

Blue is for charity and virtue; white for openness and willingness; green for freedom and eternal life. The *kurai* flower represents the seven races of the Bashkir people.

 RESPUBLIKA BURYATIYA

Blue is for the sky and water; white for purity; yellow for freedom and prosperity. The *Soembo* – the moon, sun and hearth – recall reconciliation, family life and hospitality.

 CHECHENIA

The colours of this flag represent traditional themes. Green is for Islam and also new life. Red recalls the blood shed for freedom and white is the road leading to the future.

 CHUVASHIA

The red base is the Chuvash land, from which grows the 'Tree of Life'. The three suns are an ancient Chuvash emblem. Gold is for the future and prosperity.

 DAGHESTAN

The upper green stripe is for agriculture and hope. The blue stripe is for the Caspian Sea which borders the republic. Red represents fidelity and courage.

 INGUSHETIA

The stripe is for the pure intentions and actions of the people and green is for nature, fertility and Islam. The 'sun' represents peace and creativity and its colour the people's struggles.

KABARDINO-
BALKARIA

The flag's colours evoke the blue sky, the white snow-capped mountains, and the green prairies of Kabardino-Balkaria. In the centre is a stylized representation of the Elbrus Mountains.

KALMYKIA

The vibrant yellow is symbolic of the faith of the people of Kalmykia and also represents the sun warming their land. The blue circle signifies the eternal road to the sacred lotus in the centre.

KARACHAY-
CHERKESSIA

Blue symbolizes peace, kind motives and quiet. Green represents nature, fertility and wealth. Red is for the warmth and unity of the people. The mountains in the centre recall the scenery of the republic.

KARELIA

The many lakes of Karelia are recalled by the central blue stripe and its vast pine forests by green. The red stripe symbolizes warmth, unity and continuing co-operation between the peoples of Karelia.

KHAKASSIA

The horizontal white, blue and red stripes are taken from the Russian national flag. The vertical green stripe is for eternal life and is charged with an ancient Khakassian solar symbol.

RESPUBLIKA
KOMI

The three colours of the flag recall the republic's northerly location in blue, its forests in green and its snows in white. They are also symbolic of virtues such as cleanliness, unity and purity.

RESPUBLIKA
MARIY EL

The colours are adapted from the Russian national flag, with altered shades to make them distinctive. The name of the republic appears below the sun emblem.

MORDVINIA

The flag of Mordvinia was adopted in 1995, and has the same colours as the Russian flag. In the centre is the sun emblem also found on the flags of Mariy El and Udmurtia.

NORTH OSSETIA

White symbolizes spirituality and cleanliness of intentions. Yellow represents the region's farming. The red stripe recalls both the Aryan people and their militant spirit in pursuit of freedom.

TUVA

The original Tuvan flag adopted in 1918 was also blue, yellow and white. Today, the colours are said to represent courage and strength in blue, prosperity in yellow and purity in white.

YAKUTIA

The flag recalls the blue sky and shining sun. Beneath is a white stripe recalling the snow. Red is for courage and constancy; green is for the forests of Yakutia.

RESPUBLIKA TATARSTAN

The upper green stripe of the flag represents the majority Muslim Tatar population of Tatarstan. The lower red stripe is for the Russian minority. The white fimbriation represents the peace that unites them.

UDMURTIA

The eight-pointed solar sign in the centre of the flag is said to guard the people from misfortune. The earth and stability are symbolized in black, morality and the cosmos in white, and life and the sun in red.

AZERBAIJAN

Ratio: 1:2   Adopted: 5 February 1991   Usage: National and Civil

Blue is often associated with the Turkic people

Green is the traditional colour of Islam

Red recalls European influence

Each point of the star represents a Turkic people

The colours represent the Azerbaijani motto to
'Turkify, Islamisize and Europeanize'

ASIA

AZERBAIJAN HAS BEEN under consecutive Persian,
Ottoman and Russian influence. It was part of
the USSR from 1920, until independence in 1991.

The flag dates back to the brief period of Azerbaijani independence between 1918–1920 and replaces the one used in the Soviet era. The white crescent and eight-pointed star were intentionally similar to the emblem on the Turkish flag, as Turkey has traditionally been an ally of the country. The eight points on the flag's star stand for the eight groups of Turkic-speaking peoples – the Azeris, Ottomans, Jagatais, Tatars, Kipchaks, Seljuks and Turkomans.

THE NATIONAL ARMS
The coat of arms, adopted in 1993, is set on a round shield in the colours of the flag.

ARMS OF AZERBAIJAN

The flame at the star's centre symbolizes a new era

The shield is in the colour of the national flag; blue, red and green

The star has eight points, each representing one of the eight Turkic peoples

The golden ear of corn reflects Azerbaijan's agriculture

ARMENIA

Ratio: 1:2   Adopted: 24 August 1990   Usage: National and Civil

Red recalls Armenian blood spilt during the struggle for independence

Blue is for hope and the Armenian skies

Orange represents the blessings of hard work

ASIA

ARMENIA BECAME a Soviet republic in 1922. In 1991 it gained independence from the USSR and in 1995 held its first parliamentary elections.

Armenia was independent from 1920–1921, and the flag used today comes from this era. Its origin is in a design from the Armenian Institute in Venice of 1885, although this flag used the colours red-green-blue. After independence from Russia in 1991, the Soviet flag was replaced by the 1920 tricolour of red-blue-orange.

ARMS OF ARMENIA

In 1991, the arms of 1920 replaced the Soviet coat of arms. The four emblems within the shield each represent an Armenian royal dynasty. In the centre is a stylized image of Mount Ararat. The shield is supported by an eagle and a lion, common symbols in Armenian heraldry.

ARMS OF ARMENIA

Mount Ararat, the supposed resting place of Noah's Ark, is in the centre of the arms

Four quarters of the shield represent former Armenian royal dynasties

Below the shield lie a broken leaf, a sheaf of wheat, a pen and a sword

TURKEY

Ratio: 2:3 Adopted: *5 June 1936* Usage: *National and Civil*

The star and crescent are both common symbols of the Islamic religion

One star point touches the invisible line that joins the two horns of the crescent moon

The emblems are always placed slightly towards the hoist

ASIA

FOLLOWING TURKEY'S defeat in the First World War, Mustafa Kemal Atatürk deposed the Sultan in 1922, and declared the country a republic in 1923.

Turkey's flag dates from 1844, although similar red flags were used as early as the 17th century within the Ottoman Empire. From 1920–1923, when Turkey became a republic, all the emblems of the Sultan were abolished and the flag became the main emblem.

THE CRESCENT AND STAR
Using the crescent and star emblems together is a relatively recent device, but the crescent on its own dates back to the Middle Ages. It is a symbol associated with Islam and also with Osman, the founder of the Ottoman Empire. The star first appeared on the flag in 1793. Initially it had eight points, but by the early

19th century it usually had the five seen today. In 1936, the national flag and all the other flags used in Turkey today were fully defined and specified.

A PAN-ISLAMIC SYMBOL
The crescent and star has become an emblem of the pan-Islamic movement sponsored by Turkey in the late 19th century and these symbols are now widely used on the flags and national arms of Muslim countries.

Turkey does not have a coat of arms, but there are individual flags for the President and senior members of the Turkish navy. These also contain the traditional crescent and star.

GEORGIA

Ratio: 3:5   Adopted: *14 November 1990*   Usage: *National and Civil*

Black represents Georgia's tragic past

Deep red is Georgia's national colour

White represents hope for Georgia's future

GEORGIA WAS ABSORBED into the Russian Empire in 1801 and became part of the Soviet Union in 1921. It regained independence in 1991.

The Georgian flag was chosen following a competition for a state flag in 1917 and was adopted by the country during its brief period of independence between 1918 and 1921.

THE SOVIET ERA
While part of the USSR the current flag was suppressed and Georgia flew a variation of the Red Flag (*see page 6*). This flag was adopted in 1951. It had a red field, with a thin blue stripe close to the top of the flag. In the canton it contained the traditional hammer, sickle and star emblems. However, Georgia's flag was distinct from the flags of the other Soviet Socialist Republics, in

that the hammer, sickle and star were in red, not gold. They were outlined by a blue disc, from which emanated 24 rays.

Following independence from the USSR in 1991, the 1918 flag was officially re-adopted, although with slightly modified dimensions.

THE SYMBOLISM OF THE COLOURS
The field of the flag is deep red, the Georgian national colour. When it was first adopted in 1918, the crimson represented Georgia's bright past. Today it is also said to symbolize joy. The black and white stripes of the canton are said to symbolize Georgia's tragic past and hopeful future.

LEBANON

Ratio: 1:2   Adopted: *7 December 1943*   Usage: *National*

The white band symbolizes peace

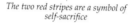

The cedar tree represents holiness, eternity and strength

The two red stripes are a symbol of self-sacrifice

ASIA

LEBANON BECAME INDEPENDENT in 1944, after 20 years as a French mandate. The country is currently rebuilding after 14 years of civil war.

The present Lebanese flag was adopted just prior to independence from France, in 1943. It was designed to be a neutral flag, not allied to any one of Lebanon's religious groups. Red is thought to be for the colour of the uniforms worn by the Lebanese Legion during the First World War. Officially the red is said to represent the people of Lebanon's sacrifice during the struggle for independence and white represents purity.

THE CEDAR OF LEBANON
Although the flag has only existed for half a century, the tree at the centre of the flag – the Cedar of Lebanon – has been an emblem

of the country since the time of King Solomon, almost 2000 years ago. Specifically, the cedar is the symbol of the country's Maronite Christian community. It first appeared on a flag in 1861 when the Lebanon was part of the Ottoman Empire. Soon after its collapse, the country became mandated to France and its flag was a French *Tricolore*, with the Cedar of Lebanon in the white band of the *Tricolore*. The cedar symbolizes happiness and prosperity for the country.

The present flag, with the cedar's foliage and trunk in green, has a variant in which the tree trunk is brown – although this is not officially recognized.

SYRIA

Ratio: 1:2   Adopted: 29 March 1980   Usage: National and Civil

The two green stars originally represented Syria and Egypt, although they are now said to represent Syria and Iraq

An earlier version of the flag had three stars, in anticipation of a union incorporating Syria, Egypt and Iraq

Red, white, black and green are pan-Arab colours

ASIA

SYRIA WAS CREATED after the dissolution of French colonial rule in 1946. From 1958–1961 it merged with Egypt to form the United Arab Republic.

In 1920, while still a French colony, Syria flew a green-white-green triband with a French *Tricolore* in the canton. At independence this was changed to a green, white and black tricolour, with three red stars for its provinces across its centre. Its current red, white and black pan-Arabic flag, was adopted when Syria became part of the United Arab Republic, but with three stars. On leaving the union in 1961, Syria briefly reverted to its original flag, before re-adopting the Arab Liberation colours in 1963.

The arms of Syria depicts the Hawk of Quraish. It is almost identical to the arms of Libya.

ARMS OF SYRIA

The shield is in the form of a national flag

The hawk was the emblem of the Quraish tribe to which the Prophet Muhammad belonged

The inscription reads – in Arabic – 'Arab Republic of Syria'

CYPRUS

Ratio: 3:5   Adopted: *16 August 1960*   Usage: *National and Civil*

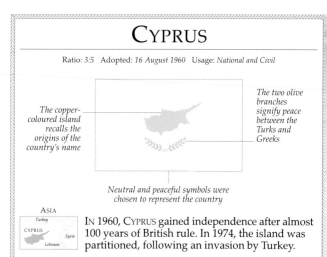

The copper-coloured island recalls the origins of the country's name

The two olive branches signify peace between the Turks and Greeks

Neutral and peaceful symbols were chosen to represent the country

ASIA

IN 1960, CYPRUS gained independence after almost 100 years of British rule. In 1974, the island was partitioned, following an invasion by Turkey.

Founded in 1193, the Kingdom of Cyprus has experienced centuries of conflict. Cyprus was conquered by the Ottoman Empire in 1571, which increased Turkish settlement on the island. It then fell under British control from 1878. The flag, adopted at independence in 1960, deliberately chose peaceful and neutral symbols in an attempt to indicate harmony between the rival Greek and Turkish communities, an ideal that has not been realized.

In 1974, Turkish forces occupied the northern part of the island, forming the 'Turkish Republic of Northern Cyprus'. The two parts of the island also fly the national flags of Greece and Turkey.

THE ISLE OF COPPER

The map of the island on the flag is supposed to be copper coloured, to express the meaning of the island's name – the Isle of Copper – but it is usually shown as yellow. The two olive branches on the white field represent peace between the two ethnic groups.

THE NATIONAL EMBLEM

Cyprus's national emblem is a dove holding an olive branch in its beak. This is a symbol of peace and reconciliation arising from the biblical story of Noah and the Ark. The dove is also symbolic of Aphrodite, the Greek goddess whose legend originated from the island.

ISRAEL

Ratio: *8:11*   Adopted: *28 October 1948*   Usage: *National*

The blue and white colours of the flag are said to be derived from the Jewish prayer shawl

The central emblem is the Star of David, which has a long association with the Jewish people

ASIA

ISRAEL WAS CREATED in 1947, following the UN Resolution (147) on Palestine. Until 1979 there were no official borders, only ceasefire lines.

The flag was designed for the Zionist movement by David Wolfsohn in 1891, over 50 years before the state of Israel was officially declared.

STAR OF DAVID
The central emblem in the form of a hexagram is known as the '*Magen David*' (Star of David), an emblem that had been used on Jewish flags for centuries before being adopted as the national flag of Israel. The blue and white colours are said to recall the colours of the *tallith* (Jewish prayer shawl). The blue is officially described as 'Yale Blue'. It is a lighter shade than used in other Israeli flags.

The merchant flag was adopted in 1948. There is also a naval ensign of similar design.

THE MERCHANT FLAG

The Star of David is slightly elongated on the merchant flag

Like other variant Israeli flags, the merchant flag is a darker shade of blue than the national flag

179

JORDAN

Ratio: *1:2*   Adopted: *16 April 1928*   Usage: *National and Civil*

The seven-pointed star represents the seven verses of Islamic belief which open the Qur'an

Red, black, green and white are pan-Arab colours

ASIA

ORIGINALLY CALLED TRANSJORDAN, as part of the Ottoman Empire, Jordan was officially renamed when independence was gained in 1946.

The colours of the Jordanian flag are those of the pan-Arab flag. They were first used in 1917 to represent 'pan-Arabianism', which sought independence from the Ottoman Empire. The star at the hoist was added in 1928, when Jordan gained nominal independence. It represents seven verses of Islamic belief.

ARMS OF JORDAN

The coat of arms is similar to that designed in 1339 for the King. The crest is a crown in his honour. The current inscription on the scroll reads 'The King of the Hashemite Kingdom of Jordan, al-Husayn-bin-Talal bin-Abdulla, Beseeches the Almighty for Aid and Success'.

ARMS OF JORDAN

The current coat of arms is very similar to that designed for King Hussein in the 14th century

The crown of His Majesty the King

The black eagle symbolizes the banner of the Messenger of God

A shield and weapons

An Arabic inscription asking for the Almighty's aid

SAUDI ARABIA

Ratio: 2:3 Adopted: 1973 Usage: *National and Civil*

A number of versions of the green flag have been used by the Wahabi sect since the 19th century

The shahada, is the Muslim Statement of Faith

Green was thought to be a favourite colour of the prophet Muhammad

ASIA

THE KINGDOM OF SAUDI ARABIA was unified under King Abd-al Aziz (ibn Sa'ud) in 1932. The Sa'ud family are the country's absolutist rulers.

The flag of Saudi Arabia symbolizes the Arab peoples of the desert. Used in various forms since the late 19th century, the green is favoured by the Wahabi sect and is believed to be the favourite colour of the prophet Muhammad.

THE *SHAHADA*.
In 1901, the *shahada,* the Muslim Statement of Faith, was added to the flag in white letters, making it one of the only national flags to contain an inscription.

By law it must be able to be read correctly – from right to left – on both sides of the flag. The sword is the symbolic sword of Abd-al-Aziz, who conquered part of Arabia in the early 20th century. It has appeared in different forms in the past, sometimes as two crossed swords.

THE SHAHADA

The inscription reads 'There is no God but Allah and Muhammad is the Prophet of Allah'

This version of the sword was added in 1981

The sword represents that given to Abd-al-Aziz by his father

YEMEN

Ratio: 2:3   Adopted: *22 May 1990*   Usage: *National and Civil*

The flag adopted for the united state was based on the common tricolour of former flags of North and South Yemen

Red, white and black are pan-Arab colours

ASIA

AFTER THREE centuries of rule by the Zaydi Imams, Yemen split into two countries in 1962. It re-united in 1990.

The first flag of the Yemen, used while the Imams were in power, was red, with a white sword placed horizontally in the centre and five white stars representing the five duties of a devout Muslim. When the two separate states were established 1962, each adopted their own flag.

SOUTH YEMEN
The flag of the People's Democratic Republic of Yemen was modelled on the Egyptian pan-Arab flag. It was a red, white and black tricolour and it bore a blue triangle, representing the Yemeni people in the hoist, while a red star represented the Socialist ruling party.

NORTH YEMEN
The flag of the Yemen Arab Republic was also modelled on the Egyptian flag. It was a red, white and black tricolour, but it was simply charged with a single, five-pointed green star in a central white band, representing Arab unity.

A UNIFIED FLAG
When the two countries were unified, the stars and the triangle were dropped, but the common elements of their flags – the pan-Arab red, white, and black stripes – were preserved for the new united flag. The new flag's pattern suggests a compromise between the officially secular south and the Islamic north.

OMAN

Ratio: 1:2   Adopted: 25 April 1995   Usage: National and Civil

The emblem of the ruling dynasty

White is for the Imam of Oman and for peace

The red field is common in the flags of the Gulf states

Green represents the mountains and fertility

ASIA

IN 1970, THE PRESENT Sultan, Qaboos bin Said, overthrew his father and renamed the country as the Sultanate of Oman.

Until 1970, Oman used the plain red banner of the indigenous people, the Kharijite Muslims. In 1970, the Sultan introduced a complete new set of national flags. Bands of green and white were added to the fly, and the national emblem, the badge of the Albusaidi Dynasty, was placed in the canton. This depicts crossed swords over a *gambia*, a traditional curved dagger.

THE SYMBOLISM OF THE COLOURS
White has been associated historically with the Imam, the religious leader of Oman and at times the political rival to the ruling Sultan. It also symbolizes peace. Green is traditionally associated with the *Jebel al Akhdar* or 'Green Mountains', which lie towards the north of the country. Red is a common colour in Gulf state flags.

THE NATIONAL EMBLEM

The national emblem is said to date back to the middle of the 18th century

A curved dagger is fastened over a pair of crossed swords

An ornate horse-bit links the weapons

UNITED ARAB EMIRATES

Ratio: 1:2   Adopted: *2 December 1971*   Usage: *National and Civil*

Green is for trees and fertility

Historically, the flags of the emirates were plain red

White symbolizes neutrality

Black represents the oil wealth of the emirates

ASIA

THE UNITED ARAB EMIRATES is an amalgamation of seven emirates, formerly known as the Trucial States, that came together in 1971.

Following a General Treaty in 1820, the seven emirates that now form the United Arab Emirates came under British protection. Red and white flags were taken up by all except the Emirate of Fujairah, a non-signatory to the treaty, which adopted a plain red flag. With minor alterations, the flags are still retained for local use. The first flag of the federation, adopted in 1968, was also red and white, but with a green star.

THE PAN-ARAB COLOURS

On independence in 1971, a flag in the pan-Arab colours – red, green, white and black – was adopted to express Arab unity and nationalism. The red also recalls the colour of the flags of the member states.

FLAG OF DUBAI

Like the other six emirates, Dubai retains its individual red and white flag

The flag colours remain constant, but the proportions have changed in recent decades

QATAR

Ratio: *11:28*   Adopted: *c 1949*   Usage: *National and Civil*

'Qatar maroon' derives from the action of sun on natural red dye

The maroon colouring and proportions
distinguish the flag from Bahrain's flag

FORMERLY LINKED TO BAHRAIN, Qatar was in a treaty relationship with Britain from 1916 until 1971, when it gained full independence.

Qatar's flag was originally plain red, like the flag of Bahrain, to which it was once linked. The peoples of both countries are Kharijite Muslims, whose traditional banner was red. The flag evolved in its present form around the middle of the 19th century, and was officially adopted when Qatar became independent from Britain in 1971.

'QATAR MAROON'
The flag's maroon colour is said to have come about from the action of the desert sun's heat on the red vegetable dyes formerly used for its flags. This colour, now known as 'Qatar maroon', was officially adopted in 1948. The nine-pointed,

zigzag, white interlock derives from a British request in the 1820s, that all friendly states around the Gulf add a white band to their flags, to distinguish them from pirate flags. During its earlier usage, before Qatar's independence, the flag also bore the name of the state in white lettering and red diamonds were placed on the white band.

THE EMBLEM OF QATAR
The circular badge of Qatar uses both the colours and serrated pattern of the flag, around its edge. In the centre is a local sailing boat, passing an island. This is set between two crossed swords. It is inscribed with the name of the state in Arabic.

BAHRAIN

Ratio: 3:5   Adopted: *c* 1932   Usage: *National and Civil*

The serrated edge was originally a straight line

*Red and white are the traditional colours
of the Gulf states*

ASIA

DESPITE IRAN'S CLAIMS of sovereignty, Bahrain, an archipelago in the Gulf, has retained its independence gained from Great Britain in 1971.

Bahrain was under British protection from 1820 to 1971. By the terms of the General Maritime Treaty of 1820, all friendly states in the Gulf undertook to add white borders to their red flags, so that they would not be taken for pirate flags. The various states of the 'Pirate Coast' then developed flags with differing white patterns on them. A plain vertical white strip was added to Bahrain's flag. In 1932 it achieved its modern form, when the line was serrated to distinguish the flag from that of Dubai.

The national arms was adopted in 1932. It is based on the colours and design of the national flag.

ARMS OF BAHRAIN

The coat of arms dates from 1932; it was designed by Sir Charles Belgrave, the Sheik's political adviser

Until independence in 1971, there was an oriental crown above the shield

The shield contains the characteristic serrated division line, as on the national flag

KUWAIT

Ratio: 1:2   Adopted: 7 September 1961   Usage: National and Civil

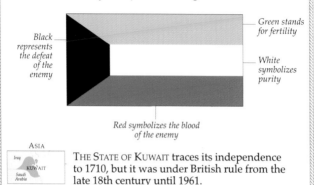

Black represents the defeat of the enemy

Green stands for fertility

White symbolizes purity

Red symbolizes the blood of the enemy

ASIA

THE STATE OF KUWAIT traces its independence to 1710, but it was under British rule from the late 18th century until 1961.

Before 1961, the flag of Kuwait, like those of other Gulf states, was red and white. The present flag is in the pan-Arab colours, but each colour is also significant in its own right. Black symbolizes the defeat of the enemy, while red is the colour of blood on the Kuwaiti swords. White symbolizes purity and green is for the fertile land. The idea for the flag's distinctive design – a horizontal tricolour with a black trapezium in the hoist – may have come from the flag used by Iraq until the late 1950s.

ARMS OF KUWAIT

The arms depicts a hawk containing an Arab *dhow* on stylized waves.

ARMS OF KUWAIT

The inscription is the name of the state

A hawk with outstretched wings

An Arab dhow – a traditional sailing boat

A shield in the national colours

IRAQ

Ratio: 2:3   Adopted: *14 January 1991*   Usage: *National and Civil*

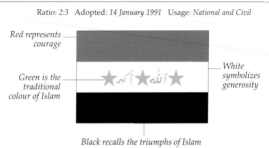

Red represents courage

Green is the traditional colour of Islam

White symbolizes generosity

Black recalls the triumphs of Islam

ASIA

ONCE PART of the Ottoman Empire, Iraq has been independent since 1932. The monarchy was overthrown and a republic proclaimed in 1958.

Since the flag of the Arab Revolt was first raised in 1917, Iraq's flag has contained the four pan-Arab colours in various guises. The colours are said to represent the qualities of those who follow Islam. Red represents courage, white stands for generosity, black is for the triumphs of Islam and green is for the religion itself. The present pattern of Iraq's flag dates from 1963 and is based on the Nasserite flag of Egypt. It was designed in anticipation of a political union with Egypt and Syria that never materialized.

THE NATIONAL ARMS

At the same time that the Nasserite flag was adopted, the golden Eagle of Saladin, another symbol of the United Arab Republic, was adopted as the national arms.

ISLAMIC VERSE

Three stars are for Iraq, Syria and Egypt

The verse reads 'Allahu Akbar' ('God is Great')

During the 1991 Gulf War, the Islamic phrase was added to the design by President Saddam Hussein

IRAN

Ratio: 4:7   Adopted: *29 July 1980*   Usage: *National and Civil*

The globe shape stands for the power of the world's downtrodden people

The sword represents strength and fortitude

Kufic script from the Qur'an

The four crescents symbolize the growth of the Muslim faith

ASIA

IRAN WAS A monarchy until 1979, when the Ayatollah Khomeini deposed the Shah. An Islamic republic was formed in 1980.

The traditional green, white and red of the Iranian flag date back to the 18th century, although there is no agreed explanation of the colours. The colours were arranged in horizontal stripes in 1906. In 1980 a new flag was introduced with the addition of emblems expressive of the Islamic Revolution.

A REVOLUTIONARY EMBLEM
The emblem in the centre of the flag is a highly stylized composite of various elements representing different facets of Islamic life: Allah, the Book, the Sword, the five principles of Islam, balance, unity, neutrality and the universal government of the downtrodden.

THE KUFIC SCRIPT
(stylized version)

A stylized version of Kufic script, used for the Qur'an

The script, repeated 22 times, is the date in the Islamic calendar on which Ayatollah Khomeini returned from exile in 1979

Along the edges of the green and red stripes appears the phrase 'Allahu Akbar' ('God is Great')

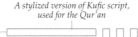

TURKMENISTAN

Ratio: 1:2   Adopted: *19 February 1997*   Usage: *National and Civil*

The wreath of olive leaves is identical to those on the United Nations flag, and was added in 1997

Each star represents one of the five Turkmen regions

Green is a colour revered in Turkmenistan

The ornamentation represents the five traditional carpet designs

ASIA

TURKMENISTAN WAS ORIGINALLY one of the 15 federated states of the USSR. It broke away and became an independent republic in 1991.

The original design of the flag was adopted on 19 February 1992, following a competition, and is based on national traditions. In the official interpretation, the five stars stand for the new regions established by the constitution of 1992. The carpet design contains five medallions or *guls*, said to represent the traditional designs used by the tribes who produced the country's famous carpets. The wreath of olive leaves was added in 1997 to 'immortalize the policy of neutrality' declared by Turkmenistan in 1995.

The coat of arms recalls the region's important agricultural products and famous horses.

ARMS OF TURKMENISTAN

The five guls from the national flag

Cotton and wheat both featured on the emblem of the former Soviet Republic of Turkmenistan

An akheltikin horse, famed in Turkmenistan

Cotton represents the country's most important agricultural product

UZBEKISTAN

Ratio: 1:2   Adopted: 18 November 1991   Usage: National and Civil

The new moon represents the new republic

There is a star for each month of the year

Blue recalls water and the sky

White denotes peace and purity

Green is symbolic of nature and fertility

Red represents the life-force in all people

ASIA

ONCE PART OF THE Mongol Empire, Uzbekistan fell to Russia in the late 19th century. It became independent from the USSR in 1991.

Uzbekistan was the first of the Central Asian republics to adopt its own non-communist national flag, although the new design is based on that of the former Soviet Uzbekistan.

The blue stripe symbolizes water and the sky. It is also the colour of the flag of Timur, who ruled an Uzbek empire in the 14th century. The white stripe is a sign of peace and purity. Green is a Muslim symbol of nature and fertility. Red is for the life-force found in all people. The new moon suggests the birth of the new republic, while the 12 stars represent the months of the Islamic calendar.

The coat of arms, adopted in 1992, is similar to the previous arms.

ARMS OF UZBEKISTAN

The arms features a bird whose outstretched wings form a crescent framing a rising sun over a landscape of mountains and rivers

Cotton is Uzbekistan's chief cash crop

Islamic crescent and star

Wheat represents the country's staple food crop

The ribbon bears the name of the state

KAZAKHSTAN

Ratio: 1:2   Adopted: 4 June 1992   Usage: National and Civil

The sky-blue field symbolizes the skies stretching over the many Kazakh people

A berkut, or steppe eagle, beneath a shining sun

The traditional 'national ornamentation' is placed close to the hoist

PART OF CENTRAL ASIA conquered by Russia in the 18th century, Kazakhstan was the last and largest republic to secede from the USSR.

Kazakhstan's post-communist flag was adopted in 1992. Its sky-blue background recalls the endless skies over the Kazakh people. It also symbolizes well-being, tranquillity, peace and unity. In the centre of the flag, below a golden sun with 32 rays, soars a bird of the species known locally as the *berkut*, or steppe eagle. Together they represent love, freedom and the aspirations of the Kazakh people. A pattern of what is described as 'national ornamentation' forms a vertical stripe near the hoist.

The new coat of arms is also based around a radiant sun. It depicts traditional features of Kazakhstan.

ARMS OF KAZAKHSTAN

The sun's rays spread out like a yurt's supporting structure

The centre of the arms is like the upper part of a yurt, the ancient felt tent of the Kazakh nomads

Winged and horned horses represent historical traditions and beliefs

MONGOLIA

Ratio: 2:1 Adopted: 1940 Usage: Civil and State

The
soyonbo
device
combines a
number of
Buddhist
emblems

Originally
the colour of
communism,
today red
represents
progress

Sky blue is the national colour of Mongolia

ASIA

Russian Federation

MONGOLIA

China

THIS REMOTE STATE has been under communist rule since 1924. The former Communist Party was democratically re-elected in 1997.

The current national flag replaced the Red flag of revolution in 1940. The red field is retained at the fly and hoist, although the colour's original socialist connotations have given way to more general themes of progress and prosperity. The sky-blue panel represents the people of Mongolia and has come to express a growing nationalism, invoking the imperial days of Genghis Khan. Despite the state's atheist stance, the flag bears a 17th-century Buddhist emblem at hoist called the *soyonbo*. The *soyonbo* comprises various ideograms representing different elements from the Buddhist view of the world.

THE SOYONBO

The tongues of the flame stand for past, present and future

The sun and moon represent ancestors of the Moguls

The vertical columns illustrate the Mongolian proverb 'Two friends are stronger than stone'

Horizontal bars indicate that vigilance is required from the highest and lowest in society

The fish stand for vigilance because fish never sleep

193

KYRGYZSTAN

Ratio: 3:5   Adopted: 3 March 1992   Usage: National and Civil

Red is for Manas the Noble, the national hero

The sun's 40 rays stand for the 40 tribes of the Kyrgyz nation

A stylized *yurt*, *the traditional home of nomadic people*

ASIA

CONQUERED BY RUSSIA under the tsars, in 1991 the Republic of Kyrgyzstan became the last of the Soviet Union Republics to declare sovereignty.

Independent since 1991, a post-communist flag was not adopted until 1992. The flag's red background is supposed to be the flag colour used by the national hero, Manas the Noble, who welded 40 tribes together to form the Kyrgyz nation.

In the centre of the flag is a yellow sun with 40 rays, representing the tribes and the legendary 40 heroes of Manas. The sun's rays run clockwise on the obverse of the flag and anti-clockwise on the reverse.

A TRADITIONAL *YURT*

At the sun's centre is a stylized bird's-eye view of the roof, or *tunduk*, of a Kyrgyz *yurt*, the traditional tent used by the nomadic

people of the steppe. It symbolizes the unity of time and space, the origin of life, hearth and home, and the history of the nomads.

ARMS OF KYRGYZSTAN

Like the arms of its neighbour, Kazakhstan, the coat of arms of Kyrgyzstan is round and does not contain a traditional shield. In the centre is a white eagle with spread wings. Behind this are snow-capped mountains, representing the mighty Tien Shan and a radiant, rising sun. This scene is bordered by wreaths of cotton and wheat, both major agricultural products in Kyrgyzstan. The name of the state is inscribed in Cyrillic script at the top.

TAJIKISTAN

Ratio: 1:2 Adopted: 24 November 1992 Usage: National and Civil

The crown and stars stand for Tajikistan's state sovereignty

White is the colour of cotton, Tajikistan's main industry

Green represents farm produce

ASIA

A FORMER MEMBER of the USSR, Tajikistan proclaimed independence in 1991, but Russian and communist influences remain strong.

In 1992, Tajikistan became the last of the former USSR republics to adopt a new flag. The red, white and green stripes are the same as those chosen in 1953 for the flag of the Tadzhik Soviet Socialist Republic. Red is the colour of the flag of the USSR; white is for cotton, Tajikistan's main export and green recalls other farm produce.

SYMBOLS OF THE NEW STATE

The centre of the flag features a gold crown and an arc of seven stars. These symbols refer to the state sovereignty of Tajikistan, friendship between all nations and the 'unbreakable union of workers, peasants and the intellectual classes' of the republic.

ARMS OF TAJIKISTAN

The new coat of arms contains many elements from the Soviet period, such as the glowing sun

Crown and stars from the national flag

Wheat and cotton, the major crops, surround the arms

Red, white and green ribbons

AFGHANISTAN

Ratio: 1:2 Adopted: 2 December 1992 Usage: National

Green represents Islam

The black stripe recalls previous flags used in Afghanistan

The arms of Afghanistan

Turkmen. Uzbek Tajik. China
AFGHANISTAN
Iran
Pakistan.

SINCE THE LAST Soviet troops pulled out of Afghanistan in 1989, civil war has meant that the country effectively has no lasting government.

Following the 1992 victory in the civil war by the *mujahideen* – the fundamentalist Muslim guerillas – the traditional black, red and green tricolour, used since 1929, was replaced by a green, white and black tricolour to which the new coat of arms, adopted with the flag in 1992, was added. The arms includes

– in Arabic – the title of the state and the Islamic creed. Islamic verses also appear on the flags or arms of Iran, Iraq and Saudi Arabia.

The black stripe recalls flags used by Afghanistan in the past and green is a symbol of the Islamic faith, prosperity and victory over imperialism.

EMBLEM OF AFGHANISTAN

A minabar *or pulpit*

The Arabic inscription reads,'There is no God but Allah and Muhammad is the Prophet of Allah'

The mosque contains a mihrab – *a niche in the mosque wall indicating the direction of Mecca*

The date, 1371 (AD 1992), is the date in Muslim calendar when mujahideen *achieved victory*

PAKISTAN

Ratio: 2:3   Adopted: 14 August 1947   Usage: National

The white strip represents non-Muslim and other minority groups in Pakistan

Star symbolizes light and knowledge

The crescent represents progress

ASIA

ONCE A PART OF **British India, Pakistan was created in 1947 as an independent Muslim state. Today, it is divided into four provinces.**

The flag was designed by Muhammad Ali Jinnah, founder of the nation. It is associated with the flag used by the All-India Muslim League as an emblem of its aim of achieving an independent Muslim state. Their flag was green, with a central white star and crescent. At independence, a white stripe was added at the hoist to represent the state's minorities.

THE SYMBOLISM OF THE COLOURS
The green and white together stand for peace and prosperity. The crescent symbolizes progress and the star represents light and knowledge.
The flag of the President is similar to the national flag. The emblems are in gold and are enclosed within a wreath of laurel. Beneath is the name of the state in Urdu.

THE PRESIDENT'S FLAG

The field of the President's flag is green and white, like the national flag

The crescent and star are symbols of Islam

The name of the state is written in Urdu

NEPAL

Ratio: 4:3 (plus border) Adopted: 16 December 1962 Usage: National and Civil

The crescent moon represents the royal house

The blue border denotes peace

Red is the colour of the rhododendron, Nepal's national flower

The sun represents the Rana family

FROM 1960 NEPAL WAS RULED by an absolute monarchy. This regime ended in 1991 when the first multiparty elections were held.

The flag of Nepal is the only national flag that is not rectangular or square. Originally, two separate triangular pennants were flown one above the other; these were then joined to form a single flag. Its crimson red is the colour of the rhododendron; the country's national flower. Red is also the sign of victory in war. The blue border is the colour of peace.

THE ROYAL STANDARD

THE SUN AND THE MOON

Until 1962, the flag's emblems, the sun and the crescent moon, had human faces. They were removed to modernize the flag. The faces remain on the sun and moon on the Royal Standard. The crescent represents the royal house and the sun denotes the Rana family, who were hereditary prime ministers until 1961.

The Royal Standard shows a rampant lion holding a lance with a flag

The sun and moon have faces, as did those on the national flag until 1962

BHUTAN

Ratio: 2:3   Adopted: *c 1965*   Usage: *National and Civil*

Saffron yellow denotes the authority of the King

The 'Thunder Dragon'

White represents purity and loyalty

Orange represents the Drukpa monasteries and religious practices

ASIA

BHUTAN IS A Buddhist state where power is shared by the king and government. The country's name in the local dialect means 'Land of the Dragon'.

In Bhutan, thunder is believed to be the voices of dragons roaring. In about 1200, a monastery was set up called the *Druk* (the 'Thunder Dragon'), with a sect called the Drukpas named after it. The name and the emblem of the dragon have been associated with Bhutan ever since. The dragon on the flag is white to symbolize purity.

TEMPORAL AND SPIRITUAL POWER
The two colours of the flag, divided diagonally, represent spiritual and temporal power within Bhutan. The orange part of the flag represents the Drukpa monasteries and Buddhist religious practice, while the saffron yellow field denotes the secular authority of the royal dynasty of the Wangchuks.

EMBLEM OF BHUTAN

The dragon symbolizes Druk, the Tibetan name for the Kingdom of Bhutan

Jewels clasped in the dragon's claws symbolize wealth

The snarling mouth expresses the strength of the male and female deities protecting the country

INDIA

Ratio: 2:3   Adopted: 22 July 1947   Usage: National

Orange represents courage and sacrifice

Green symbolizes faith and chivalry

White symbolizes peace and truth

The Chakra, *or Buddhist spinning wheel*

ASIA

UNDER BRITISH RULE from 1763, the Indian subcontinent divided into Pakistan and India in 1947 upon independence.

The national flag, adopted in 1947, is based on the flag of the Indian National Congress which was established in 1885 to press for independence. The flag's orange colour symbolizes courage and sacrifice, white stands for peace and truth, green is for faith and chivalry and blue represents the colour of the sky and the ocean.

THE *CHAKRA*
The central motif is a *Chakra*, or Buddhist spinning wheel. The 24 spokes of the wheel correspond with the 24 hours of the day, implying that there is life in movement and death in stagnation.
 The naval ensign is based on that of Britain, with the Cross of St George overall in the centre.

INDIAN NAVAL ENSIGN

The national flag is placed in the canton

The naval ensign contains the red Cross of St George

MALDIVES

Ratio: 2:3   Adopted: 26 July 1965   Usage: National and Civil

The panel of Islamic green symbolizes peace and prosperity

Red was the original colour of the Maldives flag

The crescent represents Islam

India

MALDIVES

Sri Lanka

THE ARCHIPELAGO of small islands that forms the Maldives was once a British Protectorate. The Maldives became fully independent in 1965.

Until the beginning of the 20th century the flag of the Maldives was plain red, reflecting the culture of the Arab traders from the Persian Gulf who operated among the islands. This flag remained in use after the British Protectorate was set up in 1887. The flag later acquired a white crescent facing the hoist – another sign of Islamic influence.

A NEW DESIGN

The flag was redesigned in 1948 after the independence of Ceylon (now Sri Lanka) of which the islands had been a dependency. The crescent was turned around and placed on an Islamic green panel. A pattern of black and white diagonal stripes was added along the hoist. This was dropped after independence from Britain in 1965. A modern interpretation of the colours suggests that red symbolizes the blood shed in the struggle for independence, while green stands for peace and progress.

THE NATIONAL ARMS

The coat of arms of the Maldives contains the Islamic crescent and star emblem beneath a date palm. Below the crescent is a scroll with the inscription, in Dihevi, 'State of a Thousand Islands', which recalls the many islands – over 2000 – that make up the Maldives. The crescent is flanked by two national flags.

SRI LANKA

Ratio: *1:2* Adopted: *17 December 1978* Usage: *National and Civil*

Green represents Muslims

Orange represents Hindus

The sword is a symbol of authority

The four pipul leaves are Buddhist symbols

ASIA

India

SRI LANKA

THE ISLAND OF CEYLON was a British colony until independence in 1948. It became a republic under the name Sri Lanka in 1972.

The original flag of Sri Lanka featured just the lion and sword on a red field, recalling that the Sinhalese word for lion – *'Sinhala'* – is the basis of the island's name. The flag's yellow border symbolized the protection of the nation by Buddhism.

The flag was derived from the flag of the Sinhalese kingdom of Kandy. It proved unpopular with minority groups, so vertical bands of green, for Muslims, and orange, for the Hindu Tamils, were added in 1951.

When the country's name changed from Ceylon to Sri Lanka in 1972, four leaves were added. They denote the tree under which Siddhartha sat when he received enlightenment and became the Buddha. This version of the flag was in official use from 1978.

FLAG OF KANDY

The 'Lion Flag' was the national flag of Ceylon prior to 1815 when it became a British colony

The finials are derived from the spire on top of a Buddhist temple

BANGLADESH

Ratio: 3:5 Adopted: *25 January 1972* Usage: *National*

Green represents the land

The red disc symbolizes the struggle for independence

The red circle is set slightly towards the hoist

ASIA

BANGLADESH

India *Burma*

BANGLADESH WAS FORMERLY **the eastern province of Pakistan. After a civil war with Pakistan, it became a separate country in 1971.**

The flag was originally adopted in March 1971, when the country gained independence, at which time it had a yellow silhouette map of the country in the red disc. This flag was used throughout the struggle for independence, but when the state was formally established in 1971 the outline map was omitted from the new national flag.

ARMS OF BANGLADESH
The coat of arms was adopted in 1972 and consists of the national flower, a water lily, known locally as the *shapla*, growing from stylized waves. Around it are ears of rice, and above is a sprig of jute, with four golden stars. The arms appears in the centre of the President's flag, set on a deep purple field.

THE PRESIDENT'S FLAG

Wreath of rice

A shapla (winter lily) on stylized waves

The name of the state in Bangla

A sprig of jute, with four golden stars representing nationalism, socialism, democracy and secularism

BURMA

Ratio: 2:3   Adopted: *4 January 1974*   Usage: *National and Civil*

The new socialist-style emblem was added in 1974

Red symbolizes courage

Blue represents peace

White represents purity

ASIA

In 1886, BURMA became a province of British India. It separated from India in 1937, and gained independence from British colonial control in 1948.

The flag originated in the Burman Resistance, which adopted a red flag with a white star when fighting the occupying Japanese forces during the Second World War. At independence, the star was modified to a blue canton with five small stars surrounding one large one, symbolizing the uniting of the country's diverse peoples. Red stands for the courage of the people, blue is for peace and white is for purity.

The emblem was changed in 1974 to represent the new socialist ideology in the country. The five stars were changed to 14, encircling a cog-wheel, for industry and a rice plant for agriculture.

EMBLEM OF BURMA

On the new socialist emblem, the rice stands for agriculture, while the cog-wheel represents industry

14 stars represent the unity and equality between the 14 member states of the Union

THAILAND

Ratio: 2:3   Adopted: *28 September 1917*   Usage: *National and Civil*

Red symbolizes life-blood

White stands for the purity of the Buddhist faith

The blue and white stripes were added during the First World War

Blue represents the monarchy

ASIA

Burma — Laos
India THAILAND
Cambodia

FORMERLY KNOWN AS the Kingdom of Siam, Thailand is the only Southeast Asian nation never to have been colonized.

Thailand is also known as the 'Land of the White Elephant', and this emblem appeared on its plain red flag in the 19th century. During the First World War, horizontal white stripes were added above and below the elephant.

In 1917 the elephant was abandoned, and a blue stripe was added to the middle of the flag in order to express solidarity with the Allies, whose flags were mostly red, white and blue. This flag is known as the *Trairanga* (tricolour).

The Royal Arms of Thailand was introduced in 1910. It features the *garuda*, a bird-man in Hindu mythology.

ARMS OF THAILAND

The garuda of Hindu mythology is the enemy of all things poisonous

The red garuda is placed on a field of royal yellow for the Royal Standard

LAOS

Ratio: 2:3   Adopted: *2 December 1975*   Usage: *National and Civil*

Blue represents wealth

The white disc on a blue stripe represents the full moon over the Mekong River

The white disc symbolizes unity under communism

Red symbolizes the blood shed during the struggle for freedom

ASIA

A FRENCH PROTECTORATE from the end of the 19th century, Laos gained full independence in 1953. It has been under communist rule since 1975.

The national flag of Laos was adopted in 1975, when the country became a people's republic. It is one of the few communist flags that does not use the five-pointed star as an emblem. This flag replaced the original flag of Laos, which was red, with a triple-headed white elephant on a pedestal beneath a parasol. This expressed the ancient name of the country, 'Land of a Million Elephants', and dated from the 19th century.

A FLAG FOR THE REPUBLIC
From 1953 onwards, the royal government waged war with the Pathet Lao, whose flag was blue with a white disc and red borders at the top and bottom. From 1973–1975, the Pathet Lao formed part of the government coalition, before assuming power directly and prompting the abdication of the king. Their flag was then adopted as the national flag.

In the centre is a white disc symbolizing the unity of the people under the leadership of the Lao People's Revolutionary Party and the country's bright future. The red stripes stand for the blood shed by the people in their struggle for freedom, and the blue symbolizes their prosperity.

The white disc on a blue background is also said to represent a full moon against the Mekong River.

CAMBODIA

Ratio: 2:3   Adopted: *29 June 1993*   Usage: *National and Civil*

The famous temple of Angkor Wat has appeared in various forms on Cambodia's flag

Red and blue are traditional colours

ASIA

CAMBODIA WAS A French Protectorate until 1949 when it became nominally independent once more. Full independence was achieved in 1953.

The flag used today is the same as that established in 1948, although since then five other designs have been employed. These have almost all made use of the image of the temple of Angkor Wat in one form or another. This famous temple site, dates from the 12th century, was built by the Mahidharapura monarchs. It has five towers, but these were not always all depicted in the stylized version used on flags. The temple also appears on the arms. The monarchy was restored in September 1993, the 1948 flag having been re-adopted in June of that year.

ARMS OF CAMBODIA

The glowing sun represents national rebirth

Angkor Wat is a symbol of the nation and its greatness

The inscription is the name of the country

VIETNAM

Ratio: *2:3* Adopted: *30 November 1955* Usage: *National and Civil*

The gold five-pointed star is for the unity of five groups of workers in building socialism

Red symbolizes revolution and bloodshed

IN 1954 VIETNAM was divided into north and south. In 1976, the north finally achieved its aim of reunification under communism.

Vietnam's national flag was adopted in 1976 at the end of the Vietnam War when North and South Vietnam were reunited under the new name of the Socialist Republic of Vietnam. This flag had been used by communist North Vietnam since 1955, a year after partition.

It is basically the same as the flag used by the national resistance movement, led by Ho Chi Minh, in its struggle against the occupying Japanese forces during the Second World War.

SYMBOLISM OF THE COLOURS

The red colour of the field stands for the revolution and for the blood shed by the Vietnamese people. The five-pointed yellow star represents the unity of workers, peasants, intellectuals, youths and soldiers in the building of socialism.

ARMS OF VIETNAM

The national coat of arms, which was also re-adopted in 1976, had been used by North Vietnam since 1956. It depicts a cog-wheel, symbolic of industry, and the yellow five-pointed star of socialism, enclosed by a garland of rice – the country's main agricultural product. The name of the country is inscribed on a scroll at the base of the emblem. The symbols on both the arms and the flag were inspired by the Chinese flag.

MALAYSIA

Ratio: 1:2   Adopted: 16 September 1963   Usage: National and Civil

The blue canton represents unity of the Malaysian people

The 14 red and white stripes for the 14 states of the Federation

The crescent and star of Islam

ASIA

MALAYA BECAME independent of Britain in 1957. In 1963, the Federation of Malaysia was formed, although Singapore seceded in 1965.

The first flag of independent Malaya was based on the Stars and Stripes of the United States of America, combined with Islamic symbolism. It had 11 red and white stripes and a blue canton, like the US flag, with a gold crescent and an eleven-pointed star, traditionally associated with Islam. Both the number of stripes and points on the star denoted the 11 states of the Federation.

THREE NEW STATES

In 1963 three new states – Singapore, Sabah and Sarawak – joined the Federation to form Malaysia. To reflect this the flag was amended to 14 red and white stripes representing the 14 states. When Singapore

seceded in 1965, the flag remained unaltered. The fourteenth stripe is now said to stand for the federal district of Kuala Lumpur.

THE SYMBOLISM OF THE COLOURS

The blue canton represents the unity of the Malaysian people. The crescent is for Islam, the dominant religion. The 14 points of the star are for unity among the states of the country. Yellow is the traditional colour of the rulers of the Malay states. Red and white are also traditional colours in Southeast Asia.

The national motto appears on a scroll in the coat of arms. It is repeated in both Jawi and Roman script and means 'Unity is Strength'.

Malaysia – State flags

THE FLAGS OF THE MALAYSIAN states were mostly derived from those of the 19th century, and were originally flags of the princes or sultans.

 JOHORE

The blue field represents the government. The red canton is for the *'Hulubalang'* warrior caste, who defend the state. The crescent and star represent the ruler.

 KEDAH

Red is the traditional colour of Kedah. The sheaves of yellow padi or rice, are for prosperity. The green crescent signifies Islam and the yellow shield is for sovereignty.

 KELENTAN

The red field is symbolic of the loyalty and sincerity of the people, while the white emblem represents the ruler. Kelentan has 36 royal and official flags.

 KUALA LUMPUR

Blue is for the unity of the population of Kuala Lumpur; red for courage and vigour; white is for purity, cleanliness and beauty; yellow for sovereignty and prosperity.

 LABUAN

The colours are those of the national flag and they have the same symbolism; white recalls the purity of Buddhism and red represents the life-blood of the people.

 MELAKA

The colours and pattern are taken from the national flag. Unlike the Malaysian flag, the flag of Melaka only has one stripe of red and one of white and a five-pointed star.

 NEGERI SEMBILAN

This flag reflects the hierarchy of power in Malaysia. The yellow field symbolizes the ruler, the black triangle, the district rulers and the red triangle, the people.

PAHANG

White is for the ruler, because it can change to any other colour, reflecting how a ruler can be influenced by popular opinion. Black represents the people, standing firm.

PERAK

 PERLIS

The three stripes represent different levels of the royal family. The Sultan is evoked by white, the Raja Muda by yellow and the Raja di-Hilir by black. The latter two are junior members of the ruling family.

Yellow represents the ruler and blue represents the people. The colours are arranged as two equal horizontal stripes to signify the close co-operation that should exist between the ruler and his subjects.

 PINANG

 SABAH

Light blue represents the blue seas around the island of Pinang. White is for the peace and serenity of the state and yellow for its prosperity. The tree is the Pinang palm, after which the state is named.

The zircon blue (top stripe) is for tranquillity, white for purity and justice, red for courage, ice-blue (canton) for unity and prosperity, and royal blue for strength. The mountain is Kinabalu.

 SARAWAK

SELANGOR

Yellow is the traditional colour of Borneo, where the state lies. Red and black are from the flag of the former Raja of Sarawak. The star has nine points for the nine districts of the state.

The yellow and red quarters are symbolic of flesh and blood, the combination necessary for life. The crescent and star in the canton represent Islam, the dominant religion of the state.

 TERENGGANU

The white background stands for the Sultan. It envelopes the black field, symbolizing the people. This reflects how the Sultan provides protection around his subjects.

INDONESIA

Ratio: 2:3   Adopted: *17 August 1945*   Usage: *National and Civil*

Red
represents
the body

White
symbolizes
the soul

*The flag is based on the banner of the
13th-century Indonesian Empire*

A FORMER DUTCH COLONY, Indonesia gained
independence in 1949. Western New Guinea
(Irian Jaya) was ceded to Indonesia in 1963.

The flag is based on the banner of
the 13th-century Empire of Majahapit,
red and white being the holy colours
of Indonesia at that time. These
colours were revived in the
20th century as an expression of
nationalism against the Dutch. The
first red and white flag flew in Java
in 1928 and was adopted as the
national flag of the republic in 1945
when the country declared its
independence. The red stripe is
symbolic of physical life, while white
represents spiritual life. Together
they stand for the complete human
being, body and soul. Red and white
are also traditional colours of the
Southeast Asian nations.

ARMS OF INDONESIA

*The arms show a shield
supported by a mythical
bird, the garuda. The 17
wing-feathers and 8 tail-
feathers refer to the day
and month (17 August)
on which independence
was declared in 1945*

*The shield depicts a
buffalo head, a banyan
tree and sheaves of rice
and cotton*

*The yellow star represents
religious belief*

*The national motto means
'Unity in Diversity'*

SINGAPORE

Ratio: 2:3   Adopted: *3 December 1959*   Usage: *National and Civil*

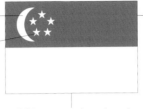

The crescent is for the new nation

The five stars symbolize ideals of democracy, peace progress, justice and equality

Red stands for universal brotherhood and equality

White represents the purity and virtue of the Singaporean people

GRANTED SELF-GOVERNMENT by Britain in 1959, Singapore became part of the Federation of Malaysia in 1963, and fully independent in 1965.

The flag dates from when Singapore became a self-governing British colony in 1959. It was preserved when Singapore joined the Malaysian Federation and adopted as the national flag when Singapore became fully independent in 1965.

The colours of red and white are those of the Malay people. Red is supposed to represent universal brotherhood and equality, while white symbolizes purity and virtue. The white crescent signifies the new nation of Singapore, while the five stars next to it represent the ideals of democracy, peace, progress, justice and equality.

The President's flag is a plain red field with the crescent and star emblem in the centre.

THE PRESIDENT'S FLAG

The President's flag simply enlarges and centres the crescent and stars motif from the national flag

Red and white represents the Malay people

BRUNEI

Ratio: *1:2* Adopted: *29 September 1959* Usage: *National and Civil*

The national emblem was placed in the centre in 1959

Black and white stripes represent Brunei's chief ministers

Yellow represents the Sultan of Brunei

ASIA

BRUNEI BECAME A **British Protectorate in 1888. It gained full independence in 1984, and is now an absolute monarchy under its Sultan.**

A similar version of this flag, without the coat of arms, was first used in 1906. The flag's main colour, yellow, is associated with the Sultan, while the black and white stripes that cut across it are the colours of the Brunei's two chief ministers. The coat of arms in the centre of the flag was added in 1959.

THE NATIONAL ARMS

The coat of arms bears testament to Brunei's Muslim traditions with the crescent, a traditional symbol of Islam, at its centre. The Arabic motto on the crescent translates as, 'Always render service by God's guidance', below it, a scroll bears the inscription '*Brunei Darussalam*' (City of Peace).

ARMS OF BRUNEI

The flag and umbrella are symbols of royalty

The crescent is symbolic of the Islamic faith

The upturned hands signify the benevolence of the government

The central mast is a symbol of the state

The inscription is the country's official title 'Brunei Darussalam'

PHILIPPINES

Ratio: 1:2 Adopted: 19 May 1898 Usage: National and Civil

The white triangle symbolizes purity and peace

Blue represents patriotism

Red symbolizes bravery

The sun and stars represent the three main areas of the country – Luzon, the Visayas and Mindanao

ASIA

THE PHILIPPINES was a Spanish colony until 1898, when it was ceded to the United States of America. It gained its independence in 1946.

The flag was first used by Filipino nationalists in exile while the Spanish still controlled the islands. When they were ceded to the USA, the Philippines became far more autonomous, and the flag was flown freely from 1898. It was banned by the Americans from 1907–1919, and the Stars and Stripes was flown exclusively on the islands.

The sun and stars are Masonic in origin. The eight rays of the sun are for the eight provinces that revolted against the Spanish. The three stars represent the country's three main geographical areas. White stands for purity and peace; red for bravery and blue for patriotism. When used at war, the red stripe is flown at the top of the flag, representing courage.

THE PRESIDENT'S FLAG

The sun is taken from the national flag

The three stars and a golden sealion were adapted from the arms of Manila

A ring of 52 white stars

TAIWAN

Ratio: 2:3   Adopted: *28 October 1928*   Usage: *National*

A blue flag with a white sun was the party flag of the Kuomingtang

Each ray represents two hours of a day

The flag is said to represent 'a white sun in a blue sky over red land'

Red recalls the Han Chinese, the dominant race in China

ASIA

TAIWAN WAS **formerly part of China. It became a separate state in 1949 under the Nationalist Party, which was expelled from government in Beijing.**

The flag adopted for Taiwan or Formosa, as it was known, had been the national flag of China. It was used from 1928–1949 when the Kuomingtang, the Chinese Nationalist Party was in power.

The red field represents China, the blue canton and white sun was the party flag of the Kuomingtang. The 12 rays of sunshine symbolize unending progress, each ray represents two hours of the day.

THE TAIPEI

This flag was adopted by Taiwan specifically for use at the Olympic Games, where its national flag was not accepted. It combines red, white and blue; the national colours of Taiwan and the Olympic emblem.

THE TAIPEI

The sun symbol is taken from the national flag

Blue, red and white are the national colours

The emblem of connected rings shows that it is an Olympic flag

CHINA

Ratio: 2:3 Adopted: 1 October 1949 Usage: National and Civil

The large star represents communism

The four smaller stars represent the social classes of the Chinese people

The red field symbolizes communist revolution and is also the traditional colour of the Chinese people

The use of five stars reflects the importance of the number five in Chinese philosophy

ASIA

CHINA HAS THE WORLD'S oldest continuous civilization. The communist Chinese People's Republic was established in 1949.

China's first national flag originated in 1872. It was yellow with a blue dragon, representing the Manchu (Qing) Dynasty which ruled China for many years. The revolt of 1911 saw the changing of the flag to five different coloured stripes. Soviet republics were established in the 1920s, each of which was represented by a red flag referring to the Soviet fatherland. The present flag dates from 1949, when the People's Republic was formed.

The large star represents communism. The red field signifies revolution and echoes the ancient Han Dynasty of 206 BC. The four stars represent the four social classes: peasants, workers, petty bourgeoisie, and patriotic capitalists.

FLAG OF HONG KONG (XIANGGANG) IN 1997

FLAG OF MACAO IN 1999

NORTH KOREA

Ratio: *1:2* Adopted: *9 September 1948* Usage: *National and Civil*

Two blue stripes stand for sovereignty, peace and friendship

The white stripes symbolize purity

Red represents communist revolution

The star is a symbol of communism

ASIA

THE KINGDOM OF KOREA was annexed by Japan in 1910. In 1948, the peninsula was partitioned into a communist north and a democratic south.

The flag was adopted in 1948, when North Korea became an independent communist state. The traditional Korean flag was red, white and blue. The regime retained these colours – with more prominence given to the red – and added a red star on a white disc. The disc recalls the Chinese yin-yang symbol, which is found on the flag of South Korea, and represents the opposing principles of nature. The red stripe expresses revolutionary traditions; while the red star is for communism.

The prominent theme of the Soviet-style coat of arms is industrialization, depicted with an electricity pylon and a large dam.

ARMS OF NORTH KOREA

The star of communism

A hydro-electric power station within a wreath of rice-ears

Industrial elements feature heavily on the arms of Korea and include a large dam and electricity pylon

The inscription on the scroll is the country's official name – The Democratic People's Republic of Korea

SOUTH KOREA

Ratio: 2:3   Adopted: *8 September 1948*   Usage: *National and Civil*

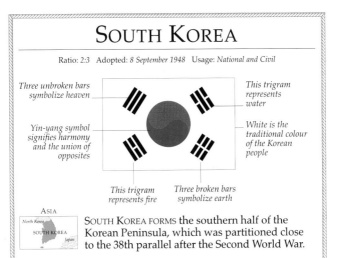

Three unbroken bars symbolize heaven

This trigram represents water

Yin-yang symbol signifies harmony and the union of opposites

White is the traditional colour of the Korean people

This trigram represents fire

Three broken bars symbolize earth

ASIA

SOUTH KOREA FORMS **the southern half of the Korean Peninsula, which was partitioned close to the 38th parallel after the Second World War.**

The flag used by the Kingdom of Korea before 1910 featured the traditional colours: red, white and blue. When South Korea separated from the north in 1948, the original flag was retained, but a few alterations were made.

A NEW SOUTH KOREAN FLAG
At the flag's centre is a disc containing an S-shaped line, the upper half being red, the lower half blue. This is derived from the Eastern yin-yang symbol, which represents the harmony of opposites in nature, for example, good and evil; male and female. When North and South Korea separated, the shape of the yin-yang was stylized in

the form of a Japanese *mon*. These are simplified versions of everyday objects, shown in symmetrical and regular forms. Yang is represented by red, and yin by blue.

The other alteration to the original flag in 1948 was to the trigrams (*kwae*) surrounding the yin-yang, which were reduced from eight to four. They are the basic trigrams from the *I-Ching*, a divination system widespread in the East. On the South Korean flag they symbolize the four polarities; heaven (upper hoist), water (upper fly), fire (lower hoist) and earth (lower fly). The white field of the flag represents peace and the white clothing traditionally worn by the Korean people.

JAPAN

Ratio: 7:10   Adopted: *27 January 1870*   Usage: *National and Civil*

The white field expresses honesty and purity

The red disc is named Hinomaru *or disc of the sun*

The sun symbol has been an element in Japan's flag's for thousands of years

ISOLATED FROM the world for centuries, Japan began to modernize in the 19th century. After defeat in the Second World War, it became a democracy.

Japan is known as 'The Land of the Rising Sun'. The Emperor of Japan and his predecessors descend from the House of Yamato, which united the country in AD 200 and they claim to be direct descendants of the sun goddess, Amaterasu Omikami.

The current flag was officially established as the national flag of Japan in 1870.

THE *HINOMARU*

The disc of the sun or *Hinomaru*, in the centre of the flag, has been an imperial badge since the 14th century. The white field stands for purity and integrity, and some suggest the red disc represents brightness, sincerity and warmth. The naval ensign is an unusual adaptation of the national flag.

JAPANESE NAVAL ENSIGN

Adopted in 1889, the naval ensign consists of the sun-disc with red rays extending to the border of the flag

Rays extend to the edge of the flag to recall the rising sun

AUSTRALIA

Ratio: *2:1*   Adopted: *22 May 1909*   Usage: *National and Civil*

The Union Jack is retained in the canton

The stars of the Southern Cross

The points of the 'Commonwealth Star' represent the members of the Federation

AUSTRALASIA & OCEANIA

THE GREAT SOUTHERN continent of Australia was unified in 1901, as a commonwealth of six formerly separate British subject states.

The first national flag was adopted in 1909 following various design competitions, but its use was restricted. It includes a blue ensign and three motifs, celebrating key aspects of Australian statehood.

THE SOUTHERN CROSS
This constellation is visible throughout the year in southern night skies and has been used as a navigational aid for centuries. It helped guide early European ships to the continent and became a popular emblem for the new settlers. The five stars of the cross appear on the fly, with seven points for the brightest stars and five for the lesser *Epsilon Crucis*.

THE UNION JACK
First flown on Australian soil by Captain Cook, it was the national flag from 1788 and remained the official citizens' land flag until 1954. It occupies the canton, denoting Australia's historical links with Great Britain.

THE 'COMMONWEALTH STAR'
This large star affirms the federal nature of government in Australia. Originally there were six points for the six federal states. The seventh point was added in 1909, to represent the Northern Territory together with the six other external territories administered by the Australian Federal Government.

Australia – State flags

THE STATE FLAGS all use the British Blue Ensign, with the state badge in the canton. The two territories do not follow this pattern.

 AUSTRALIAN CAPITAL TERRITORY

The capital territory became self-governing in 1989. The flag, adopted in 1993, depicts Canberra's city coat of arms and the Southern Cross in the city colours of blue and gold.

 NORTHERN TERRITORY

Adopted by the territory in 1978, the flag depicts the Southern Cross and a stylized Sturt's desert rose against black and ochre, which are the territorial colours.

 SOUTH AUSTRALIA

The state emblem of the piping shrike (a magpie) is shown with outstretched wings on a yellow background. The piping shrike was adopted as the flag badge in 1904.

 VICTORIA

The Royal Crown was added in 1877. The present arrangement, with the crown surmounting the Southern Cross, became the state arms in 1910.

 NEW SOUTH WALES

A gold star adorns each arm of the St George's Cross, with a golden lion *passant guardant* at the centre. This more distinctive badge replaced a previous design in 1876.

 QUEENSLAND

The state badge depicts the Royal Crown at the centre of a Maltese cross. The design of the crown was altered at the coronation of HM Queen Elizabeth II in 1952.

 TASMANIA

The Red Lion *passant* on a white background recalls historical ties with England and has remained essentially unchanged since its adoption in 1875.

 WESTERN AUSTRALIA

The Black Swan has been Western Australia's emblem since the first British colony was founded at Swan River. The flag was adopted in 1953.

PALAU

Ratio: 5:8   Adopted: *1 January 1981*   Usage: *National and Civil*

The golden disc depicts the full moon, considered by Palauans to be the best time for celebrations and harvesting

Blue symbolizes the freedom of self-rule

The full moon is set slightly towards the hoist

AUSTRALASIA & OCEANIA

UNDER US CONTROL since 1945, Palau became a republic in 1981. In 1994, it became independent in association with the United States.

The current flag was introduced in 1981 when Palau became a republic. Previously, the flag of the Trust Territory of the Pacific Islands was flown jointly with the United Nations and United States flags.

THE SYMBOLISM OF THE FLAG

The flag's very simple design belies the depth of meaning attributed to it. The explanation for the choice of colours is rooted in the history and customs of the Palauan people. The bright blue of the field, which might be assumed to be symbolic of the Pacific Ocean, is in fact a representation of the transition from foreign domination to self-government. The golden disc, which

sits slightly off centre towards the hoist, represents the full moon. The Palauans consider the full moon to be the optimum time for human activity. At this time of the month, celebrations, harvesting and planting, fishing, tree-felling, and the carving of traditional canoes are carried out. The moon is a symbol of peace, love and tranquillity.

THE SEAL OF PALAU

Palau does not have a coat of arms, but has a seal, adopted in 1981, when the country became a republic. The seal is not coloured. It depicts a traditional Palauan triangular hut, above the date of adoption. This is surrounded by the title of the state.

MICRONESIA

Ratio: *10:19*   Adopted: *30 November 1978*   Usage: *National and Civil*

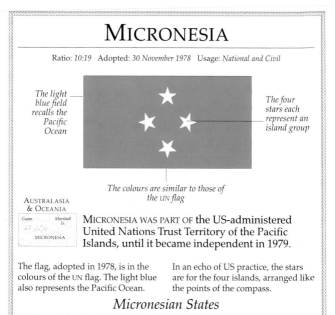

The light blue field recalls the Pacific Ocean

The four stars each represent an island group

The colours are similar to those of the UN flag

AUSTRALASIA & OCEANIA

MICRONESIA WAS PART OF the US-administered United Nations Trust Territory of the Pacific Islands, until it became independent in 1979.

The flag, adopted in 1978, is in the colours of the UN flag. The light blue also represents the Pacific Ocean.

In an echo of US practice, the stars are for the four islands, arranged like the points of the compass.

Micronesian States

CHUUK

The white coconut palm shows that the people depend on coconut resources. The white stars represent the 38 municipal units in the territory.

KOSRAE

The olive branches symbolize peace. The four stars are for the islands' four units. The *fafa* stone is traditionally used for grinding food.

POHNPEI

The six stars are for the district's six islands. The half coconut shell represents the *sakau* cup used in traditional ceremonies.

YAP

The outer and inner rings show a *rai*, a traditional symbol of unity. The white outrigger canoe symbolizes the desire to reach the goals of the state.

MARSHALL ISLANDS

Ratio: *10:19*   Adopted: *1 May 1979*   Usage: *National and Civil*

A 24-pointed star, one for each of the districts on the islands

Blue field for the Pacific Ocean

The two stripes, orange over white, represent the two parallel chains of the Marshall Islands

AUSTRALASIA & OCEANIA

THE MARSHALL ISLANDS were part of the US Trust Territory of the Pacific Islands from 1945–1986. They became fully independent in 1990.

The Marshall Islands became a self-governing territory on 1 May 1979, and on that day a new national flag was adopted. Designed by Emlain Kabua, wife of the president of the new government, it was the winning entry in a competition that had attracted 50 designs.

A FLAG FOR A PACIFIC ISLAND

The flag's dark blue field represents the vast area of the Pacific Ocean over which the islands are scattered. The star symbolizes the geographical position of the islands, which lie a few degrees above the Equator. The star has 24 points, representing the 24 municipalities of the Marshall Islands. Four of its rays extend

further than the others and stand for the capital, Majuro, and the administrative districts of Wotji, Yaluit and Kwajalein. They also form a cross, signifying the Christian faith of the Marshallese.

SYMBOLS OF PROSPERITY

The two parallel stripes extending across the flag symbolize the two parallel chains of the Marshall Islands: the Ratak (Sunrise) Chain is white, the Ralik (Sunset) Chain is orange. The stripes extend and widen upward. This is said to signify the increase in growth and vitality of life on the islands. Orange also symbolizes courage and prosperity, while white represents peace.

229

NAURU

Ratio: 1:2   Adopted: *31 January 1968*   Usage: *National and Civil*

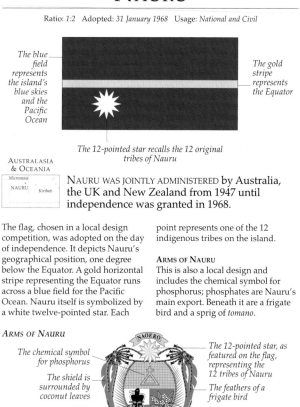

The blue field represents the island's blue skies and the Pacific Ocean

The gold stripe represents the Equator

The 12-pointed star recalls the 12 original tribes of Nauru

AUSTRALASIA
& OCEANIA

Micronesia
NAURU   Kiribati

NAURU WAS JOINTLY ADMINISTERED by Australia, the UK and New Zealand from 1947 until independence was granted in 1968.

The flag, chosen in a local design competition, was adopted on the day of independence. It depicts Nauru's geographical position, one degree below the Equator. A gold horizontal stripe representing the Equator runs across a blue field for the Pacific Ocean. Nauru itself is symbolized by a white twelve-pointed star. Each point represents one of the 12 indigenous tribes on the island.

ARMS OF NAURU

This is also a local design and includes the chemical symbol for phosphorus; phosphates are Nauru's main export. Beneath it are a frigate bird and a sprig of *tomano*.

ARMS OF NAURU

The chemical symbol for phosphorus

The shield is surrounded by coconut leaves

A frigate bird

The 12-pointed star, as featured on the flag, representing the 12 tribes of Nauru

The feathers of a frigate bird

A sprig of *tomano*

230

KIRIBATI

Ratio: *1:2*   Adopted: *12 July 1979*   Usage: *National and Civil*

The frigate bird symbolizes command of the sea

The red shield in the coat of arms also depicts a gold flying frigate bird above a rising golden sun

The blue and white wavy bands represent the Pacific Ocean

AUSTRALASIA
& OCEANIA

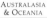

ONCE PART OF the British colony of the Gilbert and Ellice Islands, the Gilberts became independent in 1979 and adopted the name Kiribati.

Kiribati's flag is one of only three national flags which are armorial banners – flags having a design which corresponds exactly to that of the shield in the coat of arms.

ARMS OF KIRIBATI

The coat of arms dates back to May 1937 when it was granted to the Gilbert and Ellice Islands, as Kiribati and Tuvalu were then known. The shield, was then incorporated into the centre of the fly half of a British Blue Ensign as the state ensign of the colony.

Shortly before independence was granted in 1979, a local competition was held to choose a new national flag and a design based on the colonial coat of arms, was submitted to the College of Arms. The College of Arms decided to modify the design. Both the golden frigate bird and the sun were enlarged to occupy more of the top of the flag and the width of the blue and white wavy bands was reduced.

THE ORIGINAL DESIGN

However, the local people insisted on the original design, in which the top and bottom halves of the flag were equal, the sun and local frigate bird small, and the various design elements outlined in black.

The new flag was hoisted during the independence day celebrations in the capital, Tarawa on 12 July 1979.

TUVALU

Ratio: *1:2* Adopted: *1 October 1978* Usage: *National and Civil*

The Union Jack signifies continuing links with Britain

The nine stars are for the nine islands

AUSTRALASIA
& OCEANIA

THE ELLICE ISLANDS separated from the Gilbert and Ellice Islands in 1975, and adopted the name Tuvalu. Independence was gained in 1978.

Tuvalu means 'eight islands', although there are in fact nine, each of which is represented by a star on the flag. The stars' arrangement is supposed to reflect the islands' geographic distribution.

This flag was chosen because it symbolizes the continuing links with Britain and the Commonwealth.

However, anti-Commonwealth feeling rose in 1995, the government decided on a new flag without the Union Jack. The new flag introduced later that year, retained the stars, but included the arms in a triangle at the hoist. In April 1997 the original design was re-adopted, following a change of government.

ARMS OF TUVALU

The coat of arms depicts a local meeting house or maneapa

The motto means 'Tuvalu for God'

Eight sets of objects reflect the country's title, 'Eight Together'

The border contains eight sea-shells and eight banana leaves

WESTERN SAMOA

Ratio: 1:2   Adopted: *1 January 1962*   Usage: *National and Civil*

The
Southern
Cross

White
represents
purity

Red is a
traditional
Samoan
colour and
symbolizes
courage

Blue represents
freedom

AUSTRALASIA
& OCEANIA

WESTERN
SAMOA   American
Wallis &   Samoa
Futuna

UNDER THE administration of Germany, the USA
and later New Zealand, Western Samoa became
the first independent Polynesian nation in 1962.

Prior to 1899, when Samoa was
partitioned by Germany and the
USA, it was ruled by the rival
kingdoms of Malietoa and Tamasese.

The flag of Malietoa was probably
inspired by missionaries. It was a
plain red field, with a white cross
and a white star in the canton. The
rival King of Tamasese favoured the
German cause and used flags with
black crosses.

A UNITED FLAG

In 1948, by then a territory of New
Zealand, Western Samoa was
granted its current flag. This was
created jointly by the kings of
Malietoa and Tamasese. It comprised
a red field taken from the former flag

of Malietoa and the Southern Cross
from the flag of New Zealand, on a
blue field in the canton.

In 1949, the smaller fifth star was
added, making the Southern Cross
more like that on the Australian flag.
The flag was retained when
independence was granted in 1962.

ARMS OF WESTERN SAMOA

The coat of arms was adopted in
1951 and contains symbols reflecting
the Christian faith of the Samoan
people. It depicts a shield of the
Southern Cross, below a coconut
palm from the previous colonial
badge. Above the shield is a cross
recalling the national motto – 'May
God be the foundation of Samoa'.

TONGA

Ratio: 1:2   Adopted: 4 November 1875   Usage: National and Civil

The red cross represents the king's devotion to Christianity

Red represents the blood Jesus shed on the cross

White symbolizes purity

AUSTRALASIA & OCEANIA

TONGA WAS UNIFIED under King George Tupou I in 1820. In 1900, it became a British protectorate before regaining its independence in 1970.

The flag dates from 1862 when the king at the time, who had converted to Christianity in 1831, called for a national flag which would symbolize the Christian faith.

A NEW 'CHRISTIAN' FLAG

The first design was a plain white flag with a red couped cross, but this was later found to be too similar to

the International Red Cross flag, adopted in 1863, and so the white flag was placed in the canton of a red one. The cross and the red colour signify the sacrifice of Christ's blood. The 1875 constitution states that the flag shall never be altered.

The naval ensign, introduced in 1985, also has a red couped cross on white in the canton.

TONGAN NAVAL ENSIGN

Red couped cross in the canton

The naval ensign, introduced in 1985, recalls the flag of Imperial Germany

A red, cotised or bordered, Scandinavian cross

234

NEW ZEALAND

Ratio: *1:2* Adopted: *12 June 1902* Usage: *National*

The Union Jack in the canton recalls New Zealand's colonial ties to Britain

Four white-bordered red stars represent the Southern Cross

The stars all vary slightly in size

AUSTRALASIA & OCEANIA

NEW ZEALAND WAS SETTLED by the British in the 1800s and was a colony from 1841. It became a dominion in 1907 and fully independent in 1947.

New Zealand's first flag was adopted before it became a British colony. Chosen by an assembly of Maori chiefs in 1834, the flag was of a St George's Cross with another cross in the canton containing four stars on a blue field. After the formation of the colony in 1841, British ensigns began to be used.

A NEW NATIONAL FLAG
The current flag was designed and adopted for restricted use in 1869 and became the national flag in 1902. It is the British Blue Ensign, with a highly stylized representation of the Southern Cross constellation. It depicts only four of the five stars in the constellation.

Overseas Territories

COOK ISLANDS

NIUE

The 15 stars on the fly represent the 15 main islands of the group; they are arranged in a ring to indicate that each island is of equal importance.

The link with the UK is shown by the use of the Union Jack; that with New Zealand by the four stars. The large central star represents Niue itself.

INTERNATIONAL FLAGS

MANY INTERNATIONAL organizations also adopt flags, below is a selection of the most well-known.

 ARAB LEAGUE

Green was the colour of the Prophet Muhammad. The traditional crescent emblem of Islam surrounds the Muslim creed *(see page 181)*. The chain shows the Arab states united.

 ASSOCIATION OF SOUTHEAST ASIAN NATIONS

Blue is for friendship, the sky and sea. The six sheaves of rice show the six members. The yellow circle is for unity in prosperity, while the green ring is for vegetation.

 CARICOM
(Caribbean Community and Common Market)

Light blue is for the sky and dark blue for the sea. The yellow circle represents the sun. The black letters are the initials of the Caribbean Community.

 THE COMMONWEALTH

The flag depicts an outline of the world, surrounded by rays, forming the letter 'C'. Originally, there was to be a ray for each member state, but this proved impractical.

 CIS
(Commonwealth of Independent States)

This flag was adopted in 1992, it is said to represent a colonnade or a strong tree, symbolizing co-operation. The yellow sun is for light and warmth, and blue is for the sky.

 EUROPEAN UNION

The twelve stars are a notional number indicating completeness, and do not refer to the countries in the Union. It was originally adopted for the Council of Europe in 1955.

 FIAV
(International Federation of Vexillological Associations)

This flag is blue for the sky, against which flags are usually seen. The halyards, used to hoist flags, are endless, recalling the ancient origins and unknown future of flags.

NATO
(North Atlantic Treaty Organization)

Blue is for the Atlantic Ocean. The blue and white compass also evokes the ocean and symbolizes the member states of the organization on each side of it.

OLYMPIC
MOVEMENT

The five overlapping coloured rings represent the five continents joined on a field in harmony. The colours are those used on the national flags, but no specific colour represents a particular continent.

ORDER OF ST JOHN

In Britain, the flag the Order of St John is a red field with a white cross. The best-known emblem of the order is probably the Maltese cross, which appears on the flag of the order which is flown in Rome.

OAU
(Organization of African Unity)

Green represents the forest and grasslands and orange represents the deserts. White, in the centre, symbolizes peace and co-operation. The map and rings symbolize the unity of the states.

OPEC
(Organization of Petroleum-Exporting Countries)

The colours are those of the United Nations (UN), although OPEC is not a UN agency. The central white emblem is a stylized version of the agency's name. The flag was adopted in 1970.

RED CRESCENT

When the Red Cross was adopted, it was considered unacceptable in Muslim countries, so a variant flag, the Red Crescent, was designed for use in the Ottoman Empire.

RED CROSS

This flag reverses the flag of Switzerland, the home of Henri Dunant, the organization's founder. The Red Cross flag was the first flag to establish itself internationally.

SOUTH PACIFIC
COMMISSION

Blue is for the ocean. The palm represents natural resources. The 27 stars represent the member states. At first there were only eight stars, but they have increased steadily, most recently in 1983.

UNITED NATIONS
(UN)

The flag depicts a world map, centred on the North Pole. The map is surrounded by an olive wreath, symbolizing peace and co-operation. No special reason has been given for the colours.

Signal flags

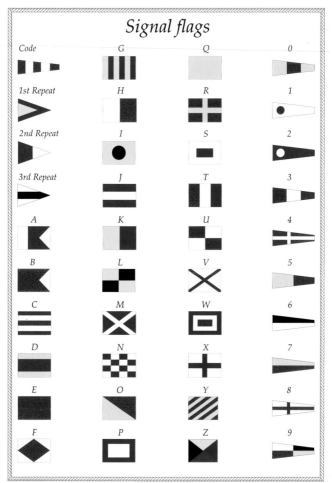

Code	G	Q	0
1st Repeat	H	R	1
2nd Repeat	I	S	2
3rd Repeat	J	T	3
A	K	U	4
B	L	V	5
C	M	W	6
D	N	X	7
E	O	Y	8
F	P	Z	9

INDEX

KEY
○ Country
❑ Overseas territory

EUROPE (see front endpaper for World Map)